The
PERSONALITY
of a CHILD
MOLESTER

The
PERSONALITY
of a CHILD
MOLESTER
An Analysis of Dreams

Alan P. Bell and Calvin S. Hall

 ALDINETRANSACTION
A Division of Transaction Publishers
New Brunswick (U.S.A.) and London (U.K.)

Second printing 2011
Copyright © 1971 by Transaction Publishers, New Brunswick, New Jersey.
Originally published in 1971 by Allan P. Bell and Calvin S. Hall.

This book is printed on acid-free paper that meets the American National Standard for Permanence of Paper for Printed Library Materials.

Library of Congress Catalog Number: 2011007163
ISBN: 978-1-4128-1847-6
Printed in the United States of America

Library of Congress Cataloging-in-Publication Data

Bell, Alan P. (Alan Paul), 1932-2002.
  The personality of a child molester : an analysis of dreams / Alan P. Bell and Calvin S. Hall.
        p. cm.
  Originally published: Chicago : Aldine, Atherton, [1971].
  ISBN 978-1-4128-1847-6
    I. Hall, Calvin S. (Calvin Springer), 1909-1985. II. Title.

RC560.C46B4 2011
616.85'836--dc22

                                                    2011007163

Acknowledgments

Perhaps the most unusual aspect of the present study is the dreamer's willingness to reveal himself to anyone. For most of his life he had viewed himself and others with profound distrust. His deepest inclination had been to hide from another's gaze, to resist others' attempts to explore his history of pain and punishment. For many years he had withdrawn from all but the most superficial contacts with other people. And yet apparently there had remained a capacity for human exchange, a determination to be known. How else are we to account for his willingness to be interviewed, to submit to psychological testing, to make public the contents of his dreams which he had first recorded on paper bags and laundry lists in surroundings which were hardly conducive to such an activity? Perhaps his cooperation in this enterprise, which appeared to offer him so little, indicated a trust in other people that his past had not entirely extinguished. Perhaps he believed that his self-disclosures would make up for what his life had been. Perhaps he was simply responding to another person's interest in him as a person, to a relationship that was less threatening than others he had known. Finally, it is possible that "our dreamer" hoped that the riddle of his existence would be solved somehow in the information he disclosed. Whatever his motivation or the degree to which it may have involved a kind of heroism, we owe "our dreamer" a special gratitude that we hope is reflected in the scope and language of our inquiry. It is to him that the present book is dedicated.

The authors also wish to thank their friends and colleagues who were kind enough to review the manuscript and to offer their helpful criticisms. These persons include Martin Weinberg, Senior Sociologist at the Institute for Sex Research, G. William Domhoff who made important editorial suggestions, and Florence Strong who helped in the scoring of the dreams and whose contribution to the study was very substantial.

CONTENTS

Personality of a Child Molester

ONE

Introduction

The present study was undertaken with two aims in mind. The first aim was to determine the relationship between what a person dreams while he is asleep and recalls in the morning and his behavior and personality in waking life. The second aim was to identify and to describe the specific variables that constitute the character of a pedophile (child molester) and to attempt to discover the origin of his sexual preoccupations and outlets.

The present study is one of a series of investigations, two of which have already been published. In the first study (Hall and Domhoff, 1968), the dreams reported by Freud and Jung in their writings were analyzed, and the results obtained from these analyses were compared with biographical and autobiographical material pertaining to the two men. In the second study (Hall and Lind, 1970), similar comparisons were made between the published dreams of Franz Kafka and his character and conduct. An added feature of the Kafka study was to compare the results of the dream analysis with a content analysis of some of his literary works. In both studies, the correspondence between dreams and waking behavior was striking. Freud, Jung, and Kafka displayed many of the same traits, interpersonal relations, preoccupations, conflicts, and complexes in their dreams as they did in waking life. In certain instances, information obtained from the dreams helped to illuminate the underlying motivations for their waking behavior.

This study differs in several respects from those conducted previously. The subject is not a famous person. He is neither a writer like Kafka nor a psychoanalyst like Freud or Jung. On the other hand, he is no ordinary person either. A more important difference is that the dreams in the present study were subjected to a content analysis without *any* knowledge of the dreamer except for his age and sex. It must be noted, however, that a certain amount of factual information is inevitably picked up from the dreams themselves. For example, it soon became apparent while reading through the dreams that the dreamer had been convicted and institutionalized for molesting children. Occasionally the dreamer's comments on a dream provided additional, outside information but these comments were rare. After the dreams were scored by two scorers (Florence Strong and Calvin Hall), Hall reported to Alan Bell the findings and the inferences drawn from them. After Bell had read this report—and before Hall was told anything about the dreamer—he raised a number of questions about the dreamer which Hall attempted to answer on the basis of the content analysis.

Another important difference between this and the previous studies was the large number of dreams that were available for the present analysis. Over a period of some three and a half years — between September, 1963 and February, 1967—the dreamer had recorded in approximately 50,000 words more than 1300 dreams. In the previous studies, only 28 of Freud's dreams, 31 of Jung's, and 37 of Kafka's, were available for the analysis which was conducted. Certainly in this respect, the present content analysis is the most ambitious ever undertaken using the system developed by Hall and Van de Castle (1966). While it is probably not necessary to use so many dreams in order to obtain a valid and reliable description of a person, the fact that there are so many recorded over a considerable length of time has made it possible to note any changes in the dreams which occurred over that period and to correlate these changes with other changes in the dreamer's life and personality.

Norman recorded his dreams from September 15, 1963, to February 8, 1967. During that period of almost three and one-half years, between the ages of 34 and 38, Norman spent approximately two years and nine months, or 80% of the time, in an institution. Although in most instances only one dream was recorded upon awakening, sometimes more than one and as many as seven different dreams were recalled the next day and entered in his diary. There were short periods of time or certain days in which Norman could not remember his dreams or failed to keep a record, but this was infrequent.

Norman's dream diary contained 1,368 dreams which could be classified and studied through a system of content analysis developed by Hall and Van de Castle (1966). This system consists of counting the number of times a particular element or class of elements appears throughout the dreams. Some of these elements are: dream characters classified by age, sex, and relationship to the dreamer; the dreamer's interactions with these characters; other activities; objects subdivided into 28 classes and subclasses; success and failure; good fortune and misfortune; and emotions. These are called *empirical* categories because they are *in* the dream reports and not derived from any particular theory of personality. *Theoretical* categories may also be formulated, but they, too, comprise elements which are in the dream reports. For example, if the dreamer dreams of breaking his leg this is scored empirically as a misfortune, but it can also be scored theoretically as castration anxiety. The dreamer's scores, treated quantitatively and converted into proportions and other indices, are then compared with those of an appropriate norm group[1] in order to determine the individual features of

1. The normative male dreams consist of five hundred reports obtained from one hundred young adult males. The results of a content analysis of these five hundred dreams are given in Hall and Van de Castle (1966). Although Norman is about fifteen years older than the average age of the norm group, this difference in age has not been found to be of great significance in determining the contents of dreams.

his dreams from which inferences regarding the dreamer's character and conduct can be drawn.

The dreams are then read through to see if there are any predominant themes that have not been identified by the Hall-Van de Castle type of scoring. During this step a search is also made for dreams in which special symbolism seems to be present. Additional inferences are then drawn from these themes and symbolic dreams.

The analysis begins with two presuppositions: first, that dreams, without free associations or amplification, or knowledge of the dreamer, shed considerable light upon the essential character structure, psychodynamics, and psychosexual development of the dreamer; second, that frequency of occurrence of a dream element or theme is a direct measure of the dreamer's preoccupation with that topic in waking life. For example, if a person has many sex dreams the prediction is made that he is also preoccupied with sex in waking life. He may engage in many sexual activities or may think a lot about sex or may read erotic books and attend erotic plays and movies.

Only after the first two steps have been taken is any attempt made to view the dream content from a theoretical perspective. In this particular study the theoretical base provided by Freudian theory has been used because it seemed to provide the kinds of constructs which were most useful in describing the dreamer's personality. In addition, an attempt has been made to explain why the dreamer is the sort of person he is as seen through his dreams. It may be objected that this is precisely what psychoanalysts and other psychotherapists who use dreams in their practice have been doing for years. The objection is well made; however, the methodology devised for this particular series of studies is quite different from that employed in the usual psychotherapeutic situation. The psychoanalyst assists the patient in interpreting elements in his dreams through the use of free associations or amplifications provided by the patient. In attempting to understand the meaning of each dream reported to him, the psychoanalyst is aided by his knowledge of the patient acquired from their long and intimate association. Inevitably, such a procedure involves a good deal of subjectivity and selectivity on the part of the therapist. Due to the requirements of psychotherapy—whose *chief* aim is to benefit the patient and not to advance science—such subjectivity and selectivity may be entirely appropriate. The aim of the present study, however, has a scientific orientation, and for that reason a reasonably objective methodology has been employed.

The last step of this particular dream analysis consisted of two parts. First, the dreams were considered chronologically in order to see if any systematic changes had occurred over the three and a half year period. Second, the implications of findings derived from this longitudinal analysis for the dreamer's future functioning have been considered.

The reader who is interested in the more technical aspects of this procedure (that is, the selection of categories, how the size of the unit to be scored is determined, the reliability of scoring, the use of norms, and so on) is referred to Hall and Van de Castle (1966), Van de Castle (1969), and Hall (1969a, 1969b). The techniques of content analysis and their various applications were the topic of a conference held in Philadelphia in 1968 (Gerbner, 1969). Another useful reference is *The General Inquirer: A Computer Approach to Content Analysis* (Stone, Dunphy, Smith, and Ogilive, 1966).

With regard to the second aim, it was believed that the unusual amount and kind of data made available to the authors offered a remarkable opportunity to explore and to explain the mind and purposes of a person whose sexual interests and activities remained something of an enigma to himself and even to the professionals who knew him. While it is impossible to view the entire range of cause-effect sequences in the life of anyone, or to see how strands of influence combine in such a way that their final outcome could have been predicted, it is possible to view in retrospect those circumstances in a person's life which reasonably relate to that person's ways of functioning. And it is this which the authors have attempted to do in the case of a person who shall hereafter be referred to as Norman (his name and all other identifying information have been changed in order to preserve Norman's anonymity).

In addition to the contents of Norman's dreams, there were other sources of information upon which we could draw. First, there was Norman's own account of himself which he gave to Bell during what could be termed an extended intake. These data included the following kinds of information: Norman's family background; his early familial experience; his relationships with others beyond the family; a history of his sexual feelings, attitudes, and behaviors; and his variety of incarcerations. While serving his psychology internship, Bell made a partially successful attempt to learn more about Norman, who was at that time hospitalized where Bell was training. It took several months for Norman to trust the relationship sufficiently that he could enter into what was for him a most unaccustomed dialogue. Although there were many other sessions, most of the information obtained from Norman in this way was gathered from approximately twenty meetings held over a seven month period, from October, 1966 through April, 1967. In the present study, direct quotations from these counseling sessions have been used wherever possible as illustrative material.

Second, there was the information provided by nine different psychological tests which were administered to Norman during the seven month period. They included the 1) Rorschach Inkblot Test, 2) Thematic Apperception Test, 3) Adjective Check List, 4) Index of Adjustment and Values, 5) Edwards Personal Preference Schedule, 6) Minnesota Multiphasic Personality Inventory, 7) Rotter Incomplete Sentences Blank-Adult Form, 8) Wechsler Adult Intelligence Scale, and 9) Study of Values. (See References, p. 124.) No more was sought from the test data than evidence of the extent to which Bell's clinical impressions of Norman were or were not confirmed. To a lesser extent, they were used by the investigator to help him in ordering those impressions according to the confidence he might have in reporting them. These psychometric data were assigned only a subsidiary role. Where only partial evidence of certain characteristics on the part of Norman was provided by tests, no efforts were made to speculate beyond that evidence.

Third, in addition to Bell's personal and test-related impressions of Norman, each of the five institutions in which Norman had been confined off and on from 1949 to 1966 was contacted for information pertaining to 1) the reasons for his admission, 2) his behaviors during the time that he was institutionalized, and 3) the diagnosis which was made. Several of these reports included diagnostic work-ups which the authors of the present study were able to compare with their own findings. This additional information also contained certain details of Norman's history which were not available elsewhere and served to make the present report more comprehensive.

The last source of data which provided the authors with information, particularly with regard to Norman's current functioning, is a series of nine letters received from Norman since September, 1967. Their contents have been used as illustrative material throughout the book, but they have also been considered as evidence of the direction in which Norman seems to be moving intrapsychically and interpersonally.

There are five different kinds of information — dreams, interviews, tests, institutional reports, and personal correspondence — but the authors have ordered and used them differentially. The dream material has been given the role of principal datum. Examples of the dream content provide the starting points in a series of considerations which forms the substance of the book. An analysis of the dream content, involving a comparison of Norman's dreams with those of the norm group as well as inferences and speculations drawn from that comparison, provides the reader with a perspective from which he may view the other data.

In the second chapter, Norman's personal history is discussed. This helps provide the reader with enough knowledge of Norman's background to understand more readily the data which are subsequently presented. In the third chapter an analysis of Norman is presented which is based upon 1) his dreams and 2) the other data derived from his waking behavior. Additional observations are offered in the fourth chapter. In the fifth chapter, impressions of the dreamer based upon the analysis of his dreams are then compared with the impressions of him which were derived from the other data, and the relationship between our findings and those of other researchers is discussed. In the sixth chapter, Norman's current adjustment is described, and an attempt is made at prognosis. The seventh and final chapter contains a description of the values of dream analysis as it has been conducted in this and other studies.

By way of summary, the present study represents an attempt to glean from a wide assortment of data the kind of evidence that helps to increase our understanding of a person whose life and whose self-revelations appeared to merit this special attention. The study has involved little collaboration on the part of the authors. In fact, it was not until two years after the project got underway that the authors met each other, and then only to reach an understanding of how the material would be presented. Hall's primary interest is in the relevance of dream analysis for investigations of human personality and behavior. Bell is primarily interested in psychosexual development and in learning more about the different ways in which people come to terms with their sexuality. It appeared that the interests of both authors could best be served in a study of this kind. Each has drawn his own inferences from the material and few efforts have been made to have their impressions of the subject coincide. Disagreements between them have not been glossed over but, rather have served as an opportunity for the authors to raise new questions about the person whom they have sought to understand as well as about their own methodologies.

TWO

Norman's Background

Norman was born in 1928 in a large Midwestern city where he grew up and attended school until the age of 15. After working at a series of jobs in order to augment the family's relatively meager income, Norman entered the United States Army in 1946 at the age of 18 and was given an honorable medical discharge 15 months later. Norman was first institutionalized in the spring of 1949 at the age of 20 and, until the age of 37, spent approximately seven years in five different mental institutions. Despite his difficulties Norman received a high school diploma through a correspondence course at the age of 23 and, when he was not in an institution, continued to live at home with his mother and sister and to work in a series of jobs in the printing field. When first seen by the senior author, Norman was 37 years old and was about to be discharged from a mental institution. He has not been institutionalized since that summer of 1966 and is presently attending college full-time.

The following account of Norman's life is given so that the reader can make better sense of the materials which follow. Where information about certain aspects of Norman's developmental history has been gathered from the dreams themselves or when it has been discussed at length in connection with the dream analysis, it has usually not been included here. This chapter is based either on personal conversations with Norman, his responses to a questionnaire, or on information from hospital records which included conversations with Norman's mother as well. From time to time certain of Norman's dreams have been included to illuminate further the experiences which are described.

Norman's maternal grandfather was German; the grandmother was Polish. A compromise of sorts was reached by speaking Polish in the home and sending their daughter—Norman's mother—to a German school. But there ends any evidence of a conciliatory spirit in the grandparents' household during the time that Norman's mother was growing up. Although her father's parents were wealthy, her father had done nothing to capitalize on these fortunate circumstances. He did not pursue his education and, even though he was a baker, he hardly ever worked because of vague ailments. His incapacity or disinclination for work, which made the family's financial condition somewhat precarious, was one of many irritants to his wife and to his daughter who also came to consider him a failure. His violent arguments with his wife were interrupted from time to time by the physical abuse of his children. His most strenuous insistence was on modesty; any evidence of sexuality on the part of his daughter was strongly censured. This was one of the few paternal attitudes which his daughter, Norman's mother, was to assimilate. He also was strict about neatness, and since his wife was not particularly tidy, arguments erupted over this. Later, their daughter, reflecting upon the familial maelstrom which she had barely survived during her childhood and adolescence, was prompted to say to her mother, "I think you could have done a better job." The mother's answer perhaps indicated otherwise. She replied, "At least we didn't kill you!"

Norman's mother went to work at the age of thirteen to help support the family. For understandable reasons she was determined not to marry. This resolution, based upon the experience she had of her parents' marriage and upon an aversion towards men whom she was inclined to associate with her father, was not kept, however. She worked some ten years in a series of menial jobs interrupted only by a period spent in a hospital recuperating from tuberculosis. At the age of twenty-four she married Norman's father, whom she soon regarded in much the same way as she had her father, and their relationship was to be a repetition of what had obtained between her parents. She was a devout member of the Roman Catholic Church; he was bitterly cynical towards religion of any kind. She was German-Polish; he was English-Irish. She was gregarious; he was a loner. She was closely involved with her children; he had resented their birth. Differences between them mounted geometrically. Her complaints that her husband was neglectful of her and the children and that he was lazy and incompetent never went unheeded. Norman's father would reply with the same temper which had already cost him many jobs. "A dignified gentleman around the neighborhood but a devil in the house," was the way Norman described him. At times he would break up the furniture—in anger towards either his wife or the landlord—and at the same time call out the window, "Stop throwing the furniture!" Once he threw a stool at his wife and injured her. These marital disagreements are reflected in Norman's dreams.

My mother was trying to clean a horse's stall, but the horse kept trying to come in so that she could not work.

Later I was looking through a window and I saw a horse running fast toward my mother. I tried to open the window to warn her, because she was looking another way. The window would not open so I put on a glove and broke the window to attract her attention. She heard me and saw the horse coming, and she was able to get out of its way.

Norman was born in 1928 at home about a year after his parents' marriage. His mother had a cold and fever at the time and, in a generally weakened condition, gave birth three weeks prematurely. Although his father had not wanted a child, on this occasion he cooperated to the extent that he procured the services of a midwife who prophesied that the boy would be strong, a prophecy based on the strength of his urinations. She also observed "as how I looked like the infant Jesus." They were living in a cold water flat not far from where his father worked in a shoe factory. He earned very little, and even the rent of ten dollars a month was not always available. Whenever they were evicted for failing to pay the rent—which was every six months—Norman's father would retaliate by damaging some portion of the landlord's property.

> I was looking out the window of my house. . . I heard an explosion. . . a dog came and took some of the burning pieces and tossed them around. I was afraid he would set the house on fire.

When Norman was eight years old his parents were separated briefly, but it was not long before his father begged to be taken back. His wife assented, for reasons perhaps unknown even to her.

Before the 1929 depression, Norman's father would become involved in fights with his fellow workers and lose whatever job he had at the time. He was no more successful working for the W.P.A. during the depression. Ultimately, he found that door-to-door selling was more suitable to his temperament. But by this time his relationship with his wife had deteriorated completely. There had been the usual arguments, the threats of separation, and finally his expulsion from the household when his wife learned that he had contracted venereal disease. Norman was twelve years old at the time and, according to his mother, he was relieved by the enforced absence of his father. As Norman now recalls, "He was more like a boarder anyway." Nine years later, when Norman was informed of his father's death, he reacted with little or no apparent emotion.

After Norman's father had been removed from the home, his mother became increasingly preoccupied with her son. Her controlling behaviors were particularly evident in Norman's relationship with his sister who had been born three years after him. He recalls, "She was always careful that my sister and I not see each other without our clothes on."

... later, I went home and asked my sister about some kind of opening. My mother said it was not important.

Whatever concerns she had became more exaggerated when Norman displayed a persistent interest in looking at his sister's genitals.

I was in a room with my sister. We were in separate beds. She showed me the lower part of her body.

... I was in a gym with other people. My sister was there. She undressed to take a shower. At first I thought she had a male organ, but as she came closer, I saw that it was only her clitoris making a bulge in her groin.

My sister was in a room. An instructor was teaching her to do some exercises. I was looking in from outside the room. My sister was nude. As she did a summersault, I saw her organ. Then she seemed to sense that she was being watched and she turned the other direction.

The reaction of Norman's mother to his interest was severe. She became increasingly restrictive with regard to their relationship, and did all that she could to reinforce the incest taboo with reference to her own relationship with her son as well as to her children's relationship.

My sister and I were in a room together, lying in separate beds.

My mother and I were sleeping in separate beds in a room. Rats were running between the beds.

Instead of extinguishing Norman's voyeurism, his mother's reaction seems to have served only to heighten his preoccupation. It did not help matters when, according to Norman, a stranger entered the house where they were living and attempted to molest his sister who was eight years old at the time:

"I heard her screaming. Some man came down the stairs. He looked at me, and then he left."

Norman claims that this incident piqued his curiosity about girls—"how they were constructed"—despite his mother's and sister's obvious irritation:

"As far as they were concerned, sex was nasty. My sister would never let me see her. In fact it wasn't until the Army that I had any idea that there was such a thing as a clitoris."

This enforced ignorance is perhaps reflected in Norman's incestuous wishes that went beyond the voyeuristic interests he had initially with respect to his sister.

I was standing next to my sister. Her body was slender and her features were beautiful. Her skin was soft and pale white. My mother and a strange woman about 35 years old were nearby. My sister came near and rested her shoulders in my left arm. My sister looked lovingly and caressingly at me, and she seemed to want me to kiss her, so I did. As we kissed, she seemed to feel a little guilty, and I supposed it was because we were brother and sister. But she did not move away. I was dressed in pajamas, and my fly felt as though it were open. I felt a tingle in my organ, and I looked down intending to close my fly. My sister thought I wanted her to touch my organ, so she put her hand on it. When she touched my organ, I felt uneasy, as though the pleasure of the embrace had been spoiled.

There were other areas of tension in Norman's childhood. There was the fact that his sister was somewhat re-tarded—"obese, lazy, dull in thinking due to a sluggish gland." This meant that she was a special object of her parents' time and attention. Norman's support was also enlisted. He was asked to give his sister every consideration, to help her with her studies, to refrain from teasing her, to do all that he could to lessen the usual distress of a child's interpersonal environment. Apparently, to Norman at least, his efforts were not entirely appreciated: "My mother has always said that I should have helped my sister more."

During his elementary school years Norman did fairly well academically. Outside of school he spent most of his leisure hours by himself at home where he would practice the violin and work with chalk at his blackboard. He had few friends, and in fact over the years became more and more an object of ridicule among his peers. The high school years, in an all-male parochial school, were passed a little more easily. He spent a good deal of time bicycling with his only friend or playing the tuba in the school band or at home reading dog stories.

"I was absorbed with dog stories, Terhune's works such as *Lad of Sunnybank*, and Jack London's *Call of the Wild*. I had lost faith in human nature, and something psychic about those dogs fascinated me."

Norman describes those years as marked with indecision over what to do vocationally, loneliness, and various internal conflicts having to do chiefly with "an attraction to sex and at the same time a fear of it."

At the age of 15, at his mother's insistence, Norman quit school and went to work. He was employed first as an elevator operator in a hospital for tubercular diseases and then for approximately one year in a printing firm where he learned how to feed the presses. Then he worked several months in a linotype shop where a buzz saw cut through one of his fingers. He left, to work on and off in four different printing establishments before he was drafted and entered the Army in 1946. He was discharged a little more than a year later on medical grounds—there were hypochondriacal complaints about his stomach—and returned home. Norman continued to work, without enthusiasm, in numerous printing firms, until his first conviction and incarceration.

Norman was twenty-one years old the first time he was committed to a state hospital. He was there six months, but the first three he does not remember:

"I actually thought I was in Hell. Once when my mother came to visit me I asked, 'what are you doing *down* here?' I thought the colored attendants were devils, and I would wrestle with them. Things didn't look real. The walls didn't look natural; it was as though they had no beginning and no end. There was one doctor I remember who put the hose in my mouth during shock treatment. He had a hard look like my father. His gaze was like my father's. There were twenty-one treatments in all, and I think as a result I can't concentrate as well as I used to." (See Chapter 3 for the symbolic significance of this episode.)

Two years later he was sent to another state hospital:

"My state of mind was different then. I had been picked up for molesting a child and sent there for observation. I remember a lot of homosexuals being there, the masculine kind. They were very aggressive and kept referring to me as 'a good lay.' I worked on the grounds, and when I didn't pass staff I ran away with another patient, but the police picked us up. I felt frustrated being there, at the idea of not being free. Besides, it wasn't doing me any good. I think I saw a psychologist exactly once. The day I passed staff, the doctor told me I'd better not come back or it would be hell. But a voice told me I'd already been in hell and it was the doctor's fault."

Nine years later, when Norman was 31 years old, he was charged with impairing the morals of a minor and admitted to a state mental institution from which he was transferred to a veterans hospital and, several months later, to a state hospital for the criminally insane:

"There I felt undignified. I would have felt more dignified if they'd put me in prison. A mental patient is like a senile person; it's as though he's not a part of society. The officers always treated the persons coming there from prison much better than those who came from hospitals. They kept referring to us as 'nuts.' I would prefer to have been called bad rather than sick."

Norman's lawyer had requested that he be sent there for observation. He could have been sent to prison for life for his felonious sex offense, but that offense was reduced to simple assault.

"The hospital was near a river. I can see it as if it were yesterday. The detectives brought me up in a station wagon alone, and I had the feeling that I'd be there forever, the same feeling I had when I was hospitalized after my first arrest."

His first sight was of buildings made from second-hand bricks. The heavy bars on the windows stood out clearly even on that misty day. Another sight which caught his attention was of the blue uniformed officers and of the criminal-patients who wore thin striped woolen shirts. The reception building where he was placed for four months was relatively new in appearance, built of yellow tile bricks. The lives of its occupants, however, were no different from what obtained in the old gray four-story buildings which surrounded it:

"We were awakened at six-thirty in the morning by someone yelling, 'Drop your cocks and grab your socks.' If you took too long dressing, someone else would yell out, 'Get your ass off the chair.' "

Orders like these were obeyed promptly, and if they were not, there was always the little private room in which one could share space with a single bed and an aluminum chamber pot. After dressing, the inmates made their beds which lined the floor eight inches apart—"the homos had a ball"—and then they were lined up for their tunnel journey to a breakfast of bread—"never toast"—hot cereal, and coffee. Fifteen to twenty minutes were allotted for this first meal of the day. At 8:00 a.m. each inmate went to occupational therapy:

"This was particularly depressing for me. I stood on a production line and made children's toys and tables and chairs out of old wooden crates. It depressed me since I'd gotten into trouble with children. And sometimes I'd think I could have been married and had children. I had a very deep feeling of what might have been."

I was confined in an institution. I was standing on a floor that felt like a bed spring, and looking through a hidden opening that led outside the institution. I tried to get through it to escape, but it was too narrow. I wanted to get out very badly, and with the force of my will I seemed to rush through the opening leaving my body inside. I went rapidly down the street. I did not know whether or not the people I passed could see me. They behaved as though they did not. I felt elated at being free. I had the form of my body but not the flesh. I passed some young girls and attractive women, and I was tempted, but I resisted. I assured myself that if I had enough will power to get through that opening without my body, then surely I had enough will power to resist that temptation.

Before proceeding with a more detailed account of Norman's life and present circumstances, we shall present the findings obtained from the two sets of data: his dreams and his waking behavior. It will be recalled that the dream analysis and the inferences drawn from it were made prior to the analyst having any information about Norman's life or waking behavior. As each aspect of Norman's personality revealed by his dreams is described, the additional information which was obtained separately about Norman is presented in order to show the extent to which a relationship exists between his dreams and his functioning in waking life.

THREE

Dreams and Personality: Independent Analyses

An analysis of Norman's 1,368 dreams reveals that all of his conflicts, confusions, concerns, preoccupations, projections, actions, and traits are expressions of an infantile character. Chronologically Norman is an adult; psychologically, he is a child, an infant, possibly even a fetus. When this is fully appreciated, then everything that can be learned from his dreams falls into place. It is the central fact of his being. The evidence of Norman's infantile personality will be considered under the following headings: 1) polymorphously perverse disposition, 2) dependency, 3) identification with children, 4) confusion of gender, 5) failure of control, 6) preoccupation with the body, 7) feminine identification, 8) fetal identification, and 9) externalized superego. In each instance, evidence from Norman's dreams is presented first, followed by the evidence obtained from conversations with him, from hospital records, from psychological tests, and from personal correspondence. Norman's own words from the dream material and the other sources are used wherever possible. The chapter concludes with a discussion of the possible reasons for Norman's infantile fixation and with an addendum in which attention is given to other questions that have a bearing on the previous discussion.

Polymorphously Perverse Disposition

DREAMS

A most important feature of Norman's infantile character is his polymorphously perverse disposition.[1] His dreams indicate a sexual involvement (either an explicit sexual encounter or sexual fantasy) with every character class except his mother, aunt, and known females.

> I was in a house with a slim, dark skinned brunette about 20. I asked her if she would have sex relations with me, and she agreed. . . .

> A child was standing on a table. I ran my hand on his buttocks. A woman came and wanted to be intimate with me and I did so.

> I was walking with a slim gray haired woman. She smiled mischievously at me and grabbed me in the crotch.

> A young boy and I became friendly and I played the passive role in an act of fellatio. . . .

> I was telling someone that a man had done pederasty with me. He told me to show him how he did it. I let down my trousers and shorts, and I inserted his penis into my rectum.

Norman has sexual interactions with or fantasies about males and females, adults, adolescents, children, babies, and animals (see Table 3.1 which shows the incidence of sexual interactions with various classes of characters).

1. This, of course, is Freud's term. Freud (1905) distinguished between deviations in respect of the sexual object and deviations in respect of the sexual aim. "Object" refers to a person or animal and "aim" refers to the nature of the sexual act. As used by Freud, the term "perversion" applies only to deviations of aim, but polymorphously perverse as we are using it here includes all varieties of sexual object choices and sexual acts.

Table 3.1. Incidence of sexual interactions with various classes of characters.

Adult sister	12
Unfamiliar adult females	59
Female adolescent	9
Female child	29
Known adult male	9
Unfamiliar adult male	16
Male adolescent	8
Male child	10
Child (sex not given)	3
Baby (sex not given)	1
Animal	2
Witnessed (Norman is not involved)	18
Grand Total	176
Total in which Norman is involved	158
All females	109
All males	43
All adults	96
All minors	60

It should be pointed out that the incidence of sex in Norman's dreams is not very much higher than the incidence of sex in the dreams of the male norm group. Male dreamers have 12 sex dreams per 100 dreams, while Norman has 13 per 100 dreams. The difference between Norman and the male population lies in the *variety* of character classes with whom Norman is erotically involved. The typical heterosexual adult male has erotic encounters almost exclusively with peer females in his dreams.

There is another difference between Norman's sexual dreams and those of the norm group. In the Hall-Van de Castle system of content analysis, five subclasses of sexual dreams are distinguished. These are (1) sexual thoughts, (2) sexual overtures, (3) erotic kissing and embracing, (4) foreplay activities, and (5) sexual intercourse. As Table 3.2 indicates, Norman has a much higher incidence of sexual thoughts, feelings, and fantasies than the norm group. This suggests that he exercises control over his sexual feelings to the extent that he does not act them out to the same degree that other males do. Norman's thinking about sex in his dreams is more similar to the erotic fantasies of a child than it is to adult sexual behavior.

Table 3.2. Incidence of various kinds of sexual activities.

Sexual interactions	Number	Norman p^1	Norms p^1
The dreamer has or attempts to have sexual intercourse with another character	27	.15	.27
The dreamer has foreplay activity, handling the sex organs, with a character	27	.15	.18
The dreamer kisses and fondles a character	13	.07	.11
The dreamer makes sexual overtures (verbal and expressive) to a character	28	.16	.30
The dreamer has sexual thoughts or fantasies about a character	81	.46	.14

p = proportion.

Norman's polymorphously perverse disposition is also indicated by the various kinds of sexual acts he engages in. He is both active and passive in his sexual encounters, and oral, anal, and genital in his sexual contacts and fantasies, as the following dreams reveal.

A patient on my ward in real life came and asked me if I would like him to massage my legs. I allowed him to massage my legs, and while he was doing it I had an emission though I tried to repress it. After he left, I felt the semen, and it felt like ear wax.

I was actively and passively intimate with another man.

I lay in bed. A teenage boy undressed and lay in the nude next to me. I was sexually excited. Then a boy about 9 years old came and lay nude on the older boy's back with his back to that of the older boy. I rubbed my lips against his groin, and he said to go ahead and stimulate his organ orally if I desired to do so. I then had an emission.

A woman had breasts but she had a male organ. I let her perform pederasty with me. We were flying in an airplane.

Norman is also openly voyeuristic and covertly exhibition-istic. The latter is indicated by appearing nude or partly clad before other people, not for the ostensible purpose of exhib-iting himself. In fact, usually he feels embarrassed when this happens. The same embarrassment is not experienced in his ubiquitous voyeuristic behaviors as the following dreams show.

I was with a young woman. She stood in front of me and bent down to raise her skirt to show me how it would look if the hem were higher.

I was in a bathroom with little girls. I paid 50 cents to a girl to show me her buttocks.

Two young girls about ten were getting into a double bed in their room. They acted as though they were feeling erotic toward each other. They decided to lie head to foot. They got under the blanket, and began to giggle. I don't recall getting into bed, but I found myself looking under the covers at them. As I watched I had an emission, and they chided me for doing it.

WAKING BEHAVIOR

At the age of seven, Norman experienced what he describes as simulated orgasms: "By holding back my urine and my bowels (in a squatting position), I experienced the sensation of an orgasm as the tension increased and the urine and feces forced its way out. There was no significant increase in the intensity of the sensation when I had my first ejaculation by masturbating at the age of nine, or later when I stimulated myself or engaged in sexual activities with another boy." In fact it would appear that no intense emotional experience accompanied Norman's first ejaculation although he can recall feeling mildly uneasy, guilty, perhaps even disgusted at the time. Prior to that time he recalls his father molesting him when he was four years old and, at the age of eight, engaging in mutual mouth-genital contacts with another boy of the same age. These contacts lasted about a year, at which time the boy's family moved away. He can still recall the pleasant sensations which accompanied these activities. At the same age he remembers having a one-sided romantic affair for six months with a girl in his neighborhood. When he suggested that they explore each other's bodies, she reported this to her mother who became so upset that the next time she saw Norman, she poured water over him. Norman, forbidden to have any kind of association with the girl, believes that the incident left him with feelings of inadequacy in his relations with members of the opposite sex. His experience of "guilt for having committed an 'unpure act' and thereby meriting hell" left him "disenchanted with sex, both homosexual and heterosexual." During the same period and until he was ten years old he can recall "romantic feelings toward my sister, who was five years old, which were equally frustrating."

Since that time Norman has engaged in masturbation (at

the present time he masturbates twice a month, reaching orgasm with this technique only four times a year) and has experienced nocturnal emissions (currently about twice a year). It would appear that even this private eroticism which does not involve the many problematic areas of interpersonal engagement is somewhat threatening to Norman:

"I try to fight off masturbation because I think it's psychologically unhealthy. It makes for negative thinking. It is easy for it to possess you, to overwhelm you, and when it does it hampers your creative ability. After I masturbate I feel completely exhausted."

His fantasies during these times are chiefly heterosexual:

"I think of a woman, and I assume the masculine role with her. I try to make it a mystical experience." He accounts for this need by the fact that he was born in November: "Pure sex is repulsive to a Scorpio. Even though a Scorpio may be frustrated without sex, it must be bound with an intellectual experience. Sensual pleasure is not the ultimate."

Norman has also been involved in mutual masturbation, active and passive fellatio and active and passive anal intercourse with other males. He has found these experiences, most of which occurred during the times that he was living in an all-male setting, pleasant. Although Norman has participated in homosexual behaviors, the extent of his real homosexual interests is reflected only in the moderate fears he has of others' homosexual interests in him. At least on one occasion he has had sexual contact with an animal.

Before one concludes that the range of sexual experience on Norman's part is unusual, it would probably be helpful to compare it with that of other males in the general population. Approximately 74 per cent of high school educated males have had nocturnal emissions by age 18; 40 per cent have experienced prepubertal heterosexual play, usually involving the exhibition of genitalia; 38 per cent have engaged in homosexual activity during the preadolescent years, and 50 per cent of males who remain single until age 35 engage in this activity during and after adolescence (it is not at all unusual for such persons to assume both the active and passive roles during such encounters); over 15 per cent of high school educated males have had sexual contacts with animals. What makes Norman's sexual history unusual is not its variety but its lack of activity. He masturbates to orgasm much less frequently than other males of his age and marital status. He has one-half to one-third the number of nocturnal emissions of other males his age. Norman has never engaged in necking, petting, or coitus with a female, even though he now describes himself as a "one" on the Kinsey scale (mainly heterosexual with a small degree of homosexuality in terms of his sexual interests and behaviors). On one occasion, at the instigation of a fellow soldier, he went to a prostitute and could not conclude the sexual act. As he puts it, "I could never enjoy the company of members of the opposite sex without fearful feelings."

Probably the outstanding feature of Norman's sexual expression is his compulsive voyeurism which, as the following letter makes clear, is directly related to his pedophilic activities:

March 9, 1969

. . . As far back as I can recall, I have had a morbid yet fascinating curiosity about the female genitals. Perhaps at the start it was not a morbid kind of curiosity. I believe that the strict rule of modesty that my Roman Catholic mother enforced was in part the reason that it developed into a morbid preoccupation. One of my earliest recollections is my longing to see my sister's genitals. I knew that she would not break my mother's rule of modesty. My desire grew more intense as time went on. I was about eight years old and my sister was five when the desire began to be an obsession. About that time, I recall a girl about my age who lived nearby. One day, two other boys my age, the girl and I were playfully wrestling. The boys and the girl got into a position where the lower parts of their bodies were facing me. The girl was wearing a dress. I tried to gently pull down her panties, but just as I had them down she felt me and struggled up saying,

"Hey, someone pulled down my panties!" I did not admit doing it, but I felt embarrassed because I thought they suspected me. I also felt frustrated from the abortive attempt. It was also about that time that I was friendly with a girl—I believe it was the same girl—and I would sit with her on her front lawn. The day it happened is blurry to me. But a few days later, as my sister and I passed under her window, her mother threw a bucket of water on me. My mother went to her house, and my sister recalls that the girl's mother said that I asked her daughter to go into her basement and show me her genitals. My mother and her began pulling hair and the police were called. That woman made me feel like a freak, a monster.

I recall the summers during those years between eight and twelve, how I sat in front of the swings in the playgrounds and stared longingly up the dresses of the girls.

When I was in the eighth grade at the school I attended, there was a girl named Mary—who sat behind me. I recall dropping my eraser so that I could look up her skirt as I picked it up.

My first recollection of seeing the female genitals was when I was 22 years old. It was the summer following my release in October, 1949 from . . . State Hospital, and my memory was recovering from the effects of the shock treatments.

On this summer day, I was walking through a secluded wooded area. A boy about 4 years old was leading a girl about three. As they stopped near me, I took the girl in my arms and I said, "Let me see it!" I moved her body so that she was on her hands and knees with the lower portion of her body facing me. I pulled down her panties and spread the lips of her vagina and looked inside, feeling a flow of satisfaction. Then I pulled up her panties, and she ran in the direction that the boy had gone when I had approached her.

For a while, I felt satisfied, but the vision wore off, and I needed to see it again. I suppose it was then that the female genitals became a fetish. I worked at printing plants, attended a commercial art school at night for a few months, had no social life, and whenever I met a girl in a secluded place I had to see it again, and I tried to get her confidence.

About three years later, I began taking some of my mother's and sister's clothing in the wooded areas and dressing in them. One day while dressed as a woman, I met two girls about seven years old. I told them that I was a nurse at a nearby hospital. I told them I would give them an examination "like I give at the hospital." I looked at their vaginas, and they left not suspecting they had done anything "nasty." They waved cheery good-byes to me as they left. I felt very good, because I had satisfied myself and my actions had not had any harmful influence on the girls' sexual life since they did not know that I had exploited them in any way. My mind was at peace.

About two years later, in 1957, I was taken to a police station for questioning about a girl I had approached, but the parents did not press charges and I was released. There were Tarzan movies showing at the theaters about this time, and they gave me the idea of carrying the girls and "accidentally" feeling under their panties. And that is what I did with that eight year old girl on that day in November, 1959. That is why I spent those years in confinement.

Most of Norman's contacts with children have involved a voyeuristic motif, a curiosity about little girls which he attempted to satisfy by investigating their genitals. During these times Norman would have—without the children knowing it—an erection and usually an ejaculation as well. On one occasion, however, he was charged with exposing himself to several ten year old girls.

It was not until the last incident, in which some blood was found on the little girl's panties, that Norman himself experienced alarm over his actions:

"I reached a crisis. I knew that either I would have to get rid of this condition, or else it would destroy me."

After reading a newspaper account of a child molester who had strangled a four year old girl, he states, "I knew then and there that I'd have to start facing myself. I was no longer satisfied with just looking. I had begun fondling. I was becoming more aggressive."

Norman estimates that he had "inspected" approximately thirty children between 1945 and 1960. He was arrested for these behaviors four times. Since 1960, however, Norman has not acted in this way. The resolve to which he came at that time has held. Apparently the fear which he had of his own aggression and its possible consequences had led to a determination which had never been accomplished by his years of hospitalization and imprisonment.

Dependency

DREAMS

Norman's mother appears in his dreams between four and five times more often than mothers appear in the norm group's dreams. His sister appears ten times more often than sisters appear in the dreams of the norm group. The fact that Norman is older than the norm population (39 years versus a mean age of 20 years in the norm group) makes the frequency of his dreams about his mother and sister even more unusual. He appears not to be married or to have had children because no wife or children belonging to him come into his dreams. There is a very low incidence of female friends and acquaintances in Norman's dreams, and although he dreams more often of known males (usually his fellow inmates or patients and not friends of long standing) the proportion of such characters is still well below the norm group. He never dreams about his father, the significance of which will be discussed later, nor does he dream about any other male relative. He dreams occasionally of an aunt who is a nun. Most of the characters, aside from his mother and sister, are unknown males and unknown females.

Norman's view of his interpersonal environment is much like that of a small child: the nuclear family with which he identifies, in which he feels secure, and the outside world of strangers.

My mother and sister were with me in a tunnel.

I was in a house with my mother and sister. My mother left on a trip. The woman who lived downstairs tried to persuade me to let her use our rooms, but I would not yield.

I was on the street after dark. I passed movie theatres. Famous stars were playing at a theatre I passed, but I did not enter. Instead, I went across the street where I met my sister, and we sat down together.

I was with my mother. Someone wanted me to get some things for myself. My mother said she would hold the things I was carrying.

In a large number of Norman's dreams he is left behind or misses a bus or a train and thereby becomes separated from his mother or sister. The fact that these dreams cause him to feel anxious indicates the extent to which he depends upon the nuclear family for whatever feelings of security he enjoys.

I was running for a subway with my sister. She caught it but I did not. I decided to run to the next station. After going several blocks, I discovered that I had turned left when I should have turned right. I was on a deserted street, and I felt very lonely.

My sister and I ran for a subway and I missed it. I took a bus . . . I wanted to ride to where my sister would get off the subway, but I was past the station when I left the bus. I was worried about my sister waiting for me. I called a taxi.

Norman's child-like dependency is illustrated further in the fact that when he is not dreaming of his home, he is dreaming of the equally sheltering environment of a penal institution or a hospital. Although he may appear to protest the sanctions imposed upon him by both the familial and institutional settings, his resentment probably does not exceed his dependency upon their restrictions nor his quest for an original, primordial, security.

I was confined in a strange institution. I saw a gate. I was not allowed outside, but no one was there, so I went out the gate. It was evening, and the streets were dark. There were small houses and small stores. Dogs were barking. I saw the headlights of a car behind me, and I was afraid it was someone from the institution looking for me. But it passed by me. I kept walking.

I was confined in an institution. I came to an opening that led outside. I was able to crawl through as far as my waist. I said aloud to myself, "If only I could be free!"

In Table 3.3, the proportions (p) of various kinds of characters appearing in Norman's dreams are compared with what obtains for the norm group.

Table 3.3. Various kinds of characters in dreams.

	Number	Norman p[1]	Norm p[1]
Mother	180	.104	.024
Sister	137	.079	.008
Aunt	6	.004	.023
Known males[2]	146	.087	.184
Known females[2]	7	.004	.106
Male strangers	519	.307	.270
Female strangers	375	.222	.097
Minors (under 18)	205	.122	.027
Father	0	.000	.025

1. p = proportion.
2. These known characters do not include family or relatives.

WAKING BEHAVIOR

Evidence of Norman's inordinate dependency upon his immediate family, and particularly his mother, is not difficult to find. Those outside the family had always been viewed with suspicion, if not alarm, by Norman's parents who never mixed socially and whose heated squabbles between themselves, which were overheard by the neighbors, alienated them further from those who lived in the immediate vicinity. Parental attitudes towards others were inevitably assimilated by Norman and his sister who were never encouraged to break the familial isolation by inviting other children to their home.

After Norman's father was expelled from the family, his mother's relationship with him became increasingly close-binding. Unable to communicate very much with his younger sister, and unwilling to risk rejection and ridicule by his peers, Norman came to rely upon the maternal relationship exclusively for social contact and communication. It was his mother who expressed interest in what he was doing at school. It was with his mother that he discussed his vocational aspirations. It was to his mother that he turned whenever he had personal problems. And whenever he experienced interpersonal difficulties with his peers, which was often, it was his mother who went out and fought what would become a common battle. Once, seeing a group of boys beating Norman up, she ran out of the house and punched the leader in the nose.

Most of Norman's childhood and adolescence were spent either alone or with his mother. Only occasionally did Norman ever play games with other children and then, more often than not, he came home in tears. During high school, reflecting a persistent disinclination to support Norman's interests in others outside the home, his mother discouraged him from dating and, as in other matters, Norman submitted to her directions. Norman sums it up very well when he states, "She always treated me like a child. Sometimes I feel as though I'm married to my mother."

Most of their communication has consisted of endless fears for him and their consequent prohibitions: "You'll overwork ... you'll get a nervous breakdown ... stay out of the cold or you'll catch pneumonia." In equal number are her complaints: "You go to extremes just like every other Scorpio ... You're a failure ... You've never found yourself ... Why do you waste your time with all those philosophers? I know everything they know ... Why don't you speak up for yourself? Why do you let *me* do it all the time?" It is a relationship which has tended to make Norman feel inadequate as a person and which has encouraged him to rely on his mother for the fulfillment of his needs. The earliest memory which Norman has of his mother is, then, not surprising: "Her stare, as I sat on her lap, which seemed to depict a protective omnipotence." Other descriptions which he gives of her, during the time he was growing up, coincide with that original impression. He perceived her as strong, active, present, powerful and protective. In her relationship with him, he saw her as loving, well-meaning, and somewhat over-indulgent.

Norman imagines that one day he will leave his mother's house where he has always lived except for those times that he was in the service or institutionalized. Meanwhile he manages to tune her out, but not entirely and possibly for good reason: "My relationship with my mother has kept me from acting out, thank goodness." Perhaps it has. It can probably be said with more certainty that this relationship has contributed a great deal to Norman's failure to face, much less cope with, the developmental tasks of childhood and adolescence.

Identification With Children

DREAMS

There is a high incidence of minors in Norman's dreams: four times as many as in the norm group. This might be explained in terms of his sexual attraction to minors and, thus, be understood as an object choice rather than as an identification on Norman's part with children. The data, however, seem to indicate that his sexual attraction to children is a function of his infantile disposition, that he dreams about children and has sexual relations with them because he himself is psychologically a child.

> There were giants pushing me and some other people.

> I was on a train and I found that I was going the wrong direction. I went outside between the cars to get ready to leave the train at the next station. A girl about seven greeted me from a running board about three feet above the floor. She seemed very sophisticated. . . .

It is common for children to be interested in children. Norman's interest is unusual for an adult. The extent of his interest suggests that he himself has the disposition of a child, that he views himself and others in a child's terms and from a child's perspective.

> I was walking in a strange town. Some girls about ten years old greeted me. I told them that I love children. They started to walk away and I told them, "Don't be afraid of me. I don't want to hurt a child."

> I met a little girl. We became companionable. I felt no romantic attachment to her.

> I was holding a boy about eight in my arms. The father came and I handed the boy to him.

> I met a girl about eight years old. She seemed distressed. She explained that her uncle was planning to ask her a number of personal questions about herself and her brother. I held her close to me and tried to soothe her anxiety. I felt a sincere and pure compassion toward her. I was sad because I did not see a way to save her from her uncle. She seemed to like me, and she was attractive, but I saw her only as a companion. There was no romantic attachment.

The fact that Norman has few aggressive and many friendly encounters with children indicates his ability to have positive relationships with young children, and can be considered further evidence of his identification with children. As a child in a confusing and unfamiliar world, Norman is more often the victim in an aggressive encounter and the one who is befriended in a friendly interaction than is the norm group. This style of interaction is much more likely to be found in the dreams of children than in the dreams of adults.

WAKING BEHAVIOR

In many respects Norman appears to identify more easily with children than with adults, to be more relaxed in their presence as though he shares with them a common frame of mind. It is as if it is with children that he belongs, expressed in a nostalgia about his past and in a determination to prolong that period of his life which did not involve the kinds of adult responsibilities which he finds so disagreeable. He continues to live at home, to meet his mother's expectations, to go to school, to rely exclusively on the government's disability check which he receives each month. It is a style of life which amounts to little more than a reiteration of his childhood. Given his routine, it is not difficult to understand how Norman has managed to maintain his experience of himself as a child.

There is no question but that Norman is severely alienated from the world of adults. The responses he makes to the projective tests indicate that he views adults in an extremely negative fashion. He will enter their world only grudgingly and even then withhold himself from its inhabitants. He is seriously inhibited in his outward responses to adults, over-cautious in whatever interpersonal contacts that are made. His Rorschach responses reveal great social apprehension, the result of an acute awareness of and sensitivity to adults, coupled with an inability to cope with them in a social situation. Norman is incredibly confused as to how to go about the business of being a socialized adult. Other adults are viewed as little more than occasional intrusions into a private, secretive, refuge-like world of his own. The test materials indicate that he shrinks from encounters with adults, makes himself invisible with a blandness which characterizes every aspect of his self-presentation. Confrontations of any kind are avoided; claims upon others are seldom made.

Norman's childlike perspective is indicated further in the large number and kind of animal responses to the Rorschach. They are derived from children's stories and not developed in the ways that are common for adults who see animals in the ink blots. This finding is supported by the summaries of two different psychological reports on Norman which were done in 1960 at two different hospitals. In both reports, and on the basis of his responses to the projective materials, Norman is described as basically infantile. In one of these reports the writer suggested that Norman saw women as remote, cold, and destructive, who could not be approached directly. At the same time, the writer observed, Norman also feared contacts with males because of his inability to relate to adults in general. For this reason it was children who became the non-threatening sexual objects. This view is supported somewhat by Norman's own explanation of his pedophilic interests:

"The child has no false self; the adult does. The child participates; the adult is an onlooker. Children are curious; the adult leaves well enough alone. The child is not cynical like the adult. Consciously I'm attracted to the innocence of youth, the way I used to be. I guess I'm searching for my own childhood by approaching children."

These particular perceptions and the rationale he offers for his behavior are more profound than he probably realizes. Clearly Norman prefers the child to the adult both socially and sexually, and he has managed to maintain (intrapsychically) a child's impressions of the world as well.

Confusion of Gender

DREAMS

One of the most unusual features of Norman's dreams is the attribution of male characteristics to females and vice versa. In five dreams, a female has a penis. In three of these dreams the female is Norman's sister. In one dream, a woman has a beard, and in another a woman is disguised as a man.

> I was a hospital patient going with others to a dining hall. We passed a woman's ward. They were nude. One of them smiled at me. I noticed that she had a penis protruding from inside her organ.

> A woman was standing nearby. Others were there. I needed a shave. I noticed that one of the women there had a beard.

In nine dreams, a man is dressed partly or entirely in women's clothes. In six of these nine dreams, it is Norman who wears feminine apparel. In other dreams Norman thinks he would make a magnificent woman; a male character tells

Norman that he has feminine charms; Norman's chest is protruding "almost like a woman's breast." He dreams of being transferred to a woman's ward in order to be cured.

> I was with a boy. Later, I was in a room. I dressed in a woman's dress, and I went into the next room to view myself in the mirror. The skirt had pleats in it. When I came to the mirror, I danced lightly and let the skirt twirl around my legs. I felt a thrill. . . .

> . . . then two men sat at places across the table. They seemed to be effeminate. They made effeminate gestures as they spoke. I happened to look under the table, and I noticed that one of them wore a skirt.

> I was in a place with other men. A man near me began telling me that I had feminine charms. I became angry and I told him that I have a man's body and he should leave me alone.

> I went upstairs to get a paper to give to the police. I put on a woman's hat by mistake.

These and other dreams with a similar motif provide ample evidence of Norman's concerns over gender and of the extent to which his own and others' gender status remains altogether ambiguous. His transvestism, his unrestrained voyeurism, his blending of the sexes into hermaphrodites, all are aspects of Norman's marked childlike orientation with its puzzlement concerning sex differences and anxiety over the everpresent threat of castration. To the question of whether Norman is a man or a woman, the answer is neither. Norman is undifferentiated sexually. He is still in a larval stage.

> . . . I was in a hospital, and I severed my penis. I wanted to attach it again, so I held it against the stump. Later, there was confusion among the patients, and an officer was flustered by the confusion.

> . . . There was a flooded room. An infant was there, and was crying and saying that a snake had bitten it. I picked it up and examined the bite on its foot. I looked for a nurse. People were around.

Then I wondered whether it was a boy or a girl. I started to open its clothing, but I stopped because I was embarrassed.

WAKING BEHAVIOR

Norman claims that he has always been baffled by the differences between what it means to be a male versus a female. Noting his father's favor of his sister over him, he supposed that perhaps her favored position had to do with her body and whatever made it different from his own. He believes that this is what made him so curious about her genitals. Apart from this, there were no familial behaviors in particular which could account for whatever confusion Norman experiences in this area. He cannot recall the feeling that either parent had wished he had been born a girl. Neither his mother nor his sister ever dressed him in girls' clothing, and he cannot recall any special fascination for female clothes or jewelry. The two or three occasions that he dressed in women's clothes during his sexual escapades were probably prompted more by strategic considerations (children were more likely to allow him to "inspect" them if he appeared to be a woman) than by any strong transvestistic interests.

What may be of relevance for Norman's gender confusion is the fact that he had always felt different from other boys his age. He never participated in masculine sports (although he did enjoy swimming) and much preferred artistic and scholarly pursuits. He recalls,

"I felt that I was much deeper in thought than other boys. I was more serious. Maleness seemed to be equated with light-heartedness, and it was always difficult for me to act that way. In fact, whenever the other boys acted sarcastic or flippant, I'd feel a surge of anger toward them. Whenever I was in a group of boys I was always afraid they'd ridicule me. I felt I couldn't communicate because I did not know how, though I had very deep thoughts I wanted to communicate."

Perhaps as a result of these early social relationships, a deep protest was formed against the kinds of values or images which others associated with masculine versus feminine roles:

"I used to try to prove I was a man. My mother wanted me to be more aggressive, but I couldn't pull it off. I finally came to realize that so-called 'masculinity' was a false goal. Aggressiveness and competition — where do they get you anyhow? It takes too much energy. So what if you win? It's a matter of being tops over nothing. You may be the victor, but it doesn't mean anything. Besides, reason is more important than power. Look at the dinosaur!"

Norman decided long ago that he was unfit for what others claimed was a properly masculine engagement with the world around him:

"Reason is more important than power. Intellectuality is neither masculine or feminine; its productions have an asexual quality about them. When I realized this, masculinity versus femininity ceased to be an important issue for me."

The statement more strongly expresses a wish than a fact. His bewilderment over his body and its claims as well as his gender role is best summed up in another statement which he makes:

"When I masturbate I am both male and female. I am a philosopher penetrating life's mystery as well as life penetrating (with her clitoris) my self (the philosopher) and his mystery." Although Norman has reached a compromise of sorts, it is obviously difficult for him to explain.

Failure of Control

DREAMS

It has already been noted in the discussion of sexual activities that Norman has little more sexual expression in his dreams than the norm group has. His sexual impulse does not run rampant despite its polymorphous nature. Moreover, he is less likely than the typical male to express his sexual feelings overtly. Much of his sexual expression appears to be fantasized. Whenever he cannot control either his erotic thoughts or actions, he feels badly. And he takes pride on those occasions when he can control himself.

. . . I made a resolution to resist temptations to masturbate.

I felt as though I had an orgasm, but my organ was dry. I was
happy that I had not had one. I had a saintly feeling that my body
was pure, clean, and healthy, and I had a feeling of euphoria.

The same control that Norman is capable of exercising
over his sexual impulses does not apply to the eliminative
functions. There is an enormous amount of urinating and
defecating in Norman's dreams. Virtually all of these eliminative acts take place under inappropriate circumstances, often
in public, causing Norman considerable embarrassment. Norman probably was and still may be eneuretic. He awakes
from one dream and finds urine on the sheet.

I defecated in a bucket. I was embarrassed because other men
were looking on.

I urinated on a bed where a woman was lying nearby. She complained and I finished in a pan. A little later some men came and
smelled the urine. They commented about it.

I had soiled my clothing with excrement.

I was urinating in the yard, and I was embarrassed to see a
woman at the other end. But she did not seem to notice me.

I defecated in my trousers, and it ran down my leg.

There is ample evidence of the extent to which Norman is
preoccupied with eliminative functions. Again and again
symbolic references (leaky pipes, fountains, floods,
over-flowing sinks, sewers, mud) are made to them, provid-
ing examples of a marked tendency in Norman to project
bodily processes on natural and man-made objects. It is significant that Norman's impulsivity does not extend to the oral
sphere. Eating, either actual or symbolic, rarely occurs in his
dreams. The pregenital impulses which Norman finds
difficult to control are the eliminative ones. This means that
the expulsive mode is more prominent in his makeup than
the incorporative mode. From this it would be surmised that

Norman is unable to save money, to hold a regular job, or to lead an orderly life.

A sink was overflowing. A woman walked into the room while I was urinating.

A young man was trying to stop a large pipe on the ceiling from dripping. When it stopped, another pipe began leaking.

I was on a muddy slope. Water was running down, and the ground was eroding.

A fire hydrant near the house was leaking and a faucet in a neighbor's garage was leaking. The plumbing in our house was shut off, so I urinated by the plug. A neighbor saw me and I was embarrassed. When I went back upstairs, my mother asked me if the rag was still in the plug in the sink, and I said, "No."

In connection with these eliminative dreams, there are several which bear out two of Freud's observations, namely, the equivalence of various bodily secretions, and the cloacal birth theory of children. Norman sees a relation between urine and semen, nasal mucus, and ear wax. The equation of feces with children is explicitly recognized in two dreams:

I put a piece of feces under water. It came alive and started to move away.

An experiment was taking place. The woman with whom I had spoken was told to be seated on a chair with a hole in the center of the seat. As she defecated, the feces was taken away and used for making children.

The failure of control in Norman's dreams implies a weak ego. It would appear that Norman is unable to postpone gratification or to deal realistically with the environment. When "he has to go, he has to go," no matter what the circumstances are. This lack of control over his eliminative processes (sphincter control) is one of the most primitive expressions of impulsivity that an adult can manifest and, probably more than any other feature of Norman's dreams, indicates the childlike structure of his character.

WAKING BEHAVIOR

One of Norman's earliest memories is of wetting his trousers:

"I used to hold it in in order to get a sexual feeling. Someone would make the remark that I'd wet my trousers, and this would embarrass me. Sometimes the other kids would beat me up for it. But I still kept doing it, I guess until I was about eight years old. I didn't wet my bed, however."

It was the same with defecation:

"I would hold it in and get a good feeling. Once, when I was serving at the altar, I had a bowel movement in the sacristy. I left the turd right on the floor, and when my aunt who is a nun called my attention to it, I was really embarrassed."

On another occasion Norman was dismissed from the church choir because other choir members had complained of the odor of urine coming from his clothing. Norman recalls another incident which illustrated the extent to which his disinclination to control his bladder served to alienate him from his peers:

"I was constantly teased by an older boy in the neighborhood because of my wetting. He would squirt his garden hose at my fly even when it was dry, and then he would laugh and yell, 'Norman wet his pants again!' I had a friendship with this girl, having played hide-and-seek with her and others. I met her this day on her front lawn. My trousers were wet from my urine and I tried to hide it, but she saw it and said, 'You wet your pants again.' I tried to deny it, saying that the bully boy had squirted his hose at me, but I knew that she did not believe me. That was the last time she would have anything to do with me."

What must be remembered is that Norman's "lack of control" was the result of a private eroticism, his quest for sensual pleasure, and not at all like what might be found in the child who simply disregards societal expectations or who flaunts others' requests to urinate or defecate at appropriate times and in appropriate places. In every other respect Norman was the model child, overly sensitive to others' demands. He was never a disciplinary problem at school or at home where he was both the teacher's and his mother's pet. Everything he did was done in moderation. And as an adult, the same is true of him. He rarely drinks and never smokes. He leads an almost monastic life, well-ordered in the extreme.

The only other area of his life in which one can find evidence of impulsivity or "lack of control" is in his employment history. Norman estimates that he has worked for ten different firms for periods lasting approximately eight months each, and for twenty other firms for periods of time ranging from one day to three months. Considering the fact that Norman was hospitalized during much of the time that he could have been employed, this number of job changes is unusual. Sometimes, Norman reports, he simply "wanted a change of scene." More often it would be his mother's concern about his receiving a raise that would prompt him to leave his place of employment. He could not bring himself to ask for an increase in salary. Rather than do that, he would simply not show up for work. But here again his behavior is not like that of a person who quits a position because he is dissatisfied with his salary or employer or colleagues or who is fired for his behavior on the job. Rather, it appears to have been prompted by his extreme feelings of inadequacy and by his inability to identify with persons or objects in his environment.

Preoccupation With the Body

DREAMS

References to body parts in Norman's dreams do not materially exceed those found in the norm group (.110 versus .102). Outstanding differences are to be found, however, with respect to the subcategories. In male dreams, references to the head and to the extremities exceed references to the torso and to sexual and internal organs by more than two to one. In

Norman's dreams, references to the torso and internal organs are much more frequent; the ratio of extremities and head to the rest of the body is less than one to one. Nor are Norman's proportions like those of females in whom there is a high incidence of references to the head. These proportions, indicating the percentages of references to body parts with regard to each subcategory, are reported in Table 3.4.

Table 3.4. References to Parts of Body.

	Norman	Male Norms	Female Norms
Head	.19	.32	.51
Extremities	.27	.37	.29
Torso	.26	.14	.10
Sex and Internal Organs	.28	.17	.10

This finding suggests that Norman is preoccupied with the central zone which includes the genitals and all of the important interior structures except for the brain, and the external genitalia.

It is when the body symbolism in Norman's dreams is examined that we discover just how much he projects onto his environment references to the body and its functions.

INTERIOR VERSUS EXTERIOR SPACE

Environments may be classified as indoors or outdoors. An analogy to this simple dichotomy is the distinction between inside and outside the body. And it is on this basis that the following assumption will be made: the dream environments of indoors and outdoors symbolize inside and outside the body.

The classification of objects in dreams makes it possible to distinguish between an internal and an external environment. Architectural references—houses, buildings, rooms, household objects like furniture, appliances, dishes—are inside. Reference to travel, streets and roads, regions, and nature are considered outside. It may be of dynamic significance that men generally dream more frequently than women about outside things and that women dream more than men about inside things. Of considerable interest is the fact that Norman exceeds both the male *and* the female norms in the references which are made to architecture and household articles in his dreams. In addition, his references to the outdoors are lower than those of women. See Table 3.5.

Table 3.5

	Norman	Males	Females
Architecture and House-hold	.515	.353	.421
Travel, Streets, Regions, Nature	.197	.326	.250

The reported proportions are of the total number of objects of whatever kind that are mentioned in dream reports. Over one-half of the objects mentioned in Norman's dreams pertains to architecture and household articles.

If the main assumption is correct, then these figures would suggest that Norman is more preoccupied with the inside of his body (body introversion) than is the average male or female. In his dreams, he represents himself as being in his body, or possibly in someone else's body (his mother's?). He does not stay inside, however; he is continually leaving and entering buildings.

The large number of rooms and buildings and their furnishings could, of course, be explained on the basis that during the period that he was recording his dreams Norman spent approximately eighty percent of the time in an institution. But suppose this environmental explanation were turned on its head. Is it possible that Norman's concern with interior space is responsible, in some measure, for his being in an institution? Given the nature of his sex dreams which involve sexual activities with other inmates, it is possible that Norman enjoys the opportunity an institution affords him for having sexual contacts. In addition, with regard to his pedophilia, the inside affords fewer dangerous temptations than the outside. Most of his child molesting in his dreams, and perhaps in his waking life as well, occurs outside a house or building. When Norman is in an institution, he is at least safer from these particular impulses.

Norman's unusual interest in interior space is supported further by the many references which are made in his dreams to shafts, tunnels, caves, and sewers — interior constructions usually in the earth.

> I walked through underground sewers until I came to an exit to the street.

> I was going up a narrow shaft to an upper room.

> I was walking through mud in a cave with several others. The tunnel went up and downhill.

> I was with my mother in a cavern. It had been flooded by an underground stream. There was a plant about 10 feet long across the water, but I was afraid to cross it.

> I was in a room partly below the ground. There was an entrance to what appeared to be a cave. Rows of sticks blocked the entrance. They stood upright. I broke one and looked inside.

Even when Norman is outside a building, he enters subterranean places. The high incidence of these objects does not accord readily with an environmental explanation, since Norman is neither a miner, a sewer worker, a speleologist, or any kind of underground worker. This further evidence of Norman's concern with interior space also serves to lessen the likelihood that Norman's concern is simply a reflection of his institutionalized status.

WRITING AND PRINTING AS SYMBOLS OF BODY FUNCTIONS

One of the object categories, communication, includes all forms of visual and written communications (not speech) and the means for producing and transmitting them. The incidence of communication elements in Norman's dreams is almost twice as high as the norm group's which, perhaps, reflects his interest in reading and writing and his vocation as a printer.

The psychological significance of writing has been analyzed by Thass-Thienemann (1967, 1968) through etymological and historical research. Writing has been found to be associated with ploughing, and both activities are associated with an aggressive concept of coitus. "He (Caesar) ploughed her, and she (Cleopatra) cropt." Shakespeare also provides a bridge between printing and the sex act. (Printing is from the same Latin word as press so that the term printing press is a tautology.) Shakespeare uses the verb, "to press," to mean press down in the sexual act (Romeo and Juliet). Norman also uses the word, "press," in this sense in several of his dreams.

> I was lying on my back on a bed and a woman came and pressed her belly against mine.

> I felt the nude body of a man below me. His organ was pressed against me.

Shakespeare also uses "print off" as a metaphor for a woman conceiving. "She did print your royal father off, conceiving you" (Winter's Tale). "Stamp" is applied by Shakespeare to the role played by the male in reproduction. (See also Sonnet 11 where "print" is used as a metaphor for "reproduce.")

Norman has many dreams in which references are made to the printing press.

> I was working at a printing plant. A large press was there, but I couldn't get it to operate.

> I was working on printing presses when a fly-wheel came off while a press was running. It sailed through the air above the presses.

I had disassembled a printing press when the power accidentally turned on, and the press collapsed.

A book binding was lying loose in a printing press. A middle-aged man turned on the press, and I was worried that the binding would jam the press.

I wanted to oil a printing press. A man was sitting on the press. He said to pour the oil into his mouth through a funnel. I did so, and he became ill.

I was repairing a printing press that had something dangling.

I was behind a printing press against the wall. The press started up and began to open. When the press was completely opened it would be so close to the wall that it would crush me. I awoke as the press was pressing me against the wall and crushing me. I was terrified.

It can be observed that something happens to or is wrong with the press in many instances. Even more significant, however, is the way in which Norman has endowed the press with human characteristics. It has something dangling from it, it collapses when the power is turned on; it crushes Norman against a wall. This particular feature of Norman's dream production becomes most evident in Norman's oiling of the machine by pouring oil into a man's mouth. Of possible significance is the frequent appearance of a woman, often Norman's mother, in these printing press dreams.

Probably the most famous printing press in literature is in Kafka's story, *In the Penal Colony*. It is a press which does not print on paper but on human flesh, eventually killing the victim. Kafka's story is mirrored, with less horrifying imagery, in one of Norman's dreams:

There were people writing on other people's bellies.

Finally, one may add to the sexual symbolism of writing and printing the fact that the English word, pencil, is derived from the Latin word for penis.

OTHER BODY IMAGERY

The printing press is only one object among many upon which Norman projects body imagery. His dreams, as already noted, are filled with shafts, caves, stairways, elevators, subterranean passages, sewers, hallways, corridors, basements, holes, narrow streets, and buildings.

> I was with a man. We were in the basement of a building where men were locked in a room. He said they were dead. The building was very old. We went up the elevator. I commented that the elevator shaft is like the spine in a body, and that energy can ride up and down the spine like an elevator.

> I was in prison. Guards were around. There was a hole in a fence, and I started to crawl through, but I hesitated halfway through. I helped pass some dolls through the hole.

> I was walking on a narrow street. I had to walk through a narrow alley.

> We were climbing up a shaft that resembled a dumb waiter shaft.

> There was a clothes wringer near an open shaft. The wringer went in reverse and the clothes fell down the shaft. I was upset about losing the clothing.

> I was with my mother. We had to go upstairs through a staircase and then we had to crawl up a shaft. We received my sister's newborn baby from some nuns.

The word shaft is interesting because it signifies both a solid column such as the shaft of a spear and a hollow passage such as a mine shaft. The first signification suggests the penis, while the second suggests the vagina, womb, and gastrointestinal tract. One meaning refers to something exterior to the body, and the other to interior organs. It may be noted, however, that even the penis is not solid inasmuch as it has a conduit in it. Moreover, the phallic symbolism of shaft is suggested by the etymology of the word. It is derived from a word which originally meant, "to cut with a sharp tool." This ancient meaning is close to the modern slang usage of shaft as a verb which signifies a particularly vicious, underhanded, and unwarranted attack upon someone.

Coital metaphors are common in Norman's dreams: dumping coal into a smoke stack, lightning going down a chimney, pushing a truck into a garage, and so on. The sexual significance of touching is expressed by such imagery as touching a small bird which shivers and squirms in Norman's hand, and touching a wire which causes an explosion. The phallic significance of guns is indicated by a dream in which a rifle protrudes between the legs of a woman, and another in which a gun and bullets are soaked with a white, tacky liquid. The phallic significance of dolls is expressed in a dream in which Norman has a doll about three inches long which he is trying to fix so it will excrete liquid.

> I touched a wire and there was an explosion in the house. One floor began to sag. I was sorry I had touched the wire.

> I caught a small bird. When I started to touch it, it shivered. It squirmed in my hand as I held it.

> I had a rubber doll about 3 inches long, and I was trying to fix it so that it would excrete liquid. My mother came, and I hid the doll to avoid embarrassment.

> I had a gun, some bullets, and a knife. Some white tacky liquid began flooding at my feet. The gun and bullets were soaked, but I cleaned them and loaded the gun. I did not tell anyone about the gun.

> I saw a bolt of lightning strike a building and go down the chimney flue.

An entire chapter could be written on the subject of holes in Norman's dreams. They appear in every conceivable context. His most frequent reactions to them are either to fill them up (close them) or go through them. If a hole is hypothesized to represent the vagina—and there is much linguistic support for the hypothesis, especially in slang expressions—

then Norman's reactions express an ambivalent attitude toward the female genitals, and perhaps the womb. They are either to be denied by removing them or else they are seen as a means of escape either from the womb into the external world or into the womb from the outside world. As already noted, there is a great deal of leaving and entering in Norman's dreams which would suggest an ambivalence toward the fetal state.

I was in a building that appeared to be an institution. I and other men were told to fill in some holes that were in the floor with furniture. I didn't think there was enough furniture to fill the holes and make the floor level and solid.

Big rats were coming through the walls. I plugged up the holes they had made in the walls.

There was a hole in the floor of a greenhouse that contained a herb about 10 feet high. I began filling in the hole with dirt. It was dark down there, and there were strange birds there.

I was standing on a floor that felt like a bed spring, and looking through a hidden opening that led outside the institution. I tried to get through it to escape from the institution, but it was too narrow. I wanted to get out very badly, and with the force of my will I seemed to rush through the opening leaving my body inside.

Although Norman does not use much nature imagery in his dreams, there is one very beautiful evocation of damage to the body which uses flower symbolism:

I went outside and started to pick a flower. I was stopped by a hand. When I looked up, I saw that it was my sister's hand. She said, "Don't pick the flower. You may break the bulb underneath." I decided to pick it. I did it very carefully, but the bulb broke anyway. My sister and I were very sad, and we started to cry. Then she said, "It's all right. You did the best you could." Then we held hands and tried to smile.

Is this a metaphorical representation of earlier sex play

with his sister, or is it a fantasy on the part of Norman? This dream of defloration is paralleled in another type of imagery. On another occasion he dreams of breaking the seal of an envelope and feels guilty for having done it. Given Norman's dreams of having sexual relations with his sister as well as these other dreams which may symbolize that experience, it is not at all unlikely that Norman has actually had incestuous relations with his sister.

Norman's preoccupation with the interior of his body is evidence of a childish concern. The child is fascinated by the processes of elimination and reproduction, and by what goes on within the body. We are told by Melanie Klein that the child has body destruction fantasies, by Otto Rank that he harbors the trauma of his own birth, by Sandor Ferenczi that he wishes to return to the thallistic womb, and by Freud that he fantasies where babies come from, is terrified by thoughts of castration, and already has a death instinct. The first ego, we are told, is a body ego. Norman, in this respect as well as others, is fixated at an early psychosexual stage.

WAKING BEHAVIOR

Norman's body is hardly noticeable to the person who meets him and who may only be impressed by his fragile appearance and pasty complexion. He is five feet eleven inches tall and weighs almost 170 pounds, but his slightly stooped posture and ectomorphic frame make him appear smaller and lighter than he actually is. He moves with caution, and when he is seated he appears to be physically drawn into himself. One would hardly guess from his physical appearance that Norman has come to consider his body the chief enemy, that Norman's primary interest is to renounce his body's claims and to quiet its impulses. And yet it is this determination which stands out most prominently in the present data.

It is in intellectual activity, in sometimes bewildering mental pursuits, that Norman seeks deliberately to disregard his physical existence. His intellectual curiosity is reminiscent of his sexual curiosity and illustrates very well the relationship which Freud presumed to exist between the two preoccupations, in which the former is considered a sublimation of the latter.

I want to see the forest, not just the trees. I want to focus on the really crucial questions of life. In the beginning my interest in philosophy was more like an escape. I had quit high school and was doing work I wasn't particularly interested in. I finally got to the point where the choice was either suicide or the effort to make sense of my existence. After I first got into trouble, I realized that there was so much I didn't know. I didn't want to be like the man in *Proverbs* who repeats the same error and who Solomon likened to a dog who returns to his vomit. And I have found that my intellectual pursuits are not just helpful emotionally but that they are also quite reasonable, that they have a validity quite apart from my emotional needs. When you come down to it, life has to involve the integration of intellect and emotion.

The way in which Norman has come to manage these dimensions of his life can hardly be termed an integration. It is much more a splitting off of thoughts and feelings, a deliberate disregard of a fundamental and cataclysmic portion of his existence, an utterly severe judgement of his flesh and of his feelings. As he puts it,

"I feel most alive when I'm not aware of my sexual drive and energy. Whether I fight off the drive or give in; both result in a lethargic state."

The extent to which Norman wishes to become completely unaware of his body and the enthusiasm which he had for this task is revealed in the two letters that follow:

November 15, 1969

... The physical change that I feel since I have noticeably improved my control of my psychic powers ... new information I have acquired on the subject ... is from Lobsong Rampa's autobiography titled *The Rampa Story* ... Mr. Rampa explains that the people of Tibet have enormous physiological control of their internal organs and have tremendous psychic powers. They can travel at will in their astral bodies. (In case you are unfamiliar with this function of the human being, the astral body is inside of the physical body and is attached to it by an umbilical cord connected at the base of the spine. This is why sexual energy can help develop one's ability to travel in his astral body. The umbilical cord is endless, and one can travel any distance, even to other planets. NOTICE THIS: ASTRAL TRAVEL IS NOT IMAGINATION. Mr. Rampa can travel anywhere in his astral body, through any wall, and see what is happening at any place on Earth, and he can tell you what took place when he was there.) . . . This ability to leave one's body when it is damaged or aged and enter another by means of the transplanting of one's astral body to another body that resembles it has been a fact in Tibet for centuries, along with the other psychic powers that are possible. It makes the West—with its heart transplants—look like child's play. There is no "eternal Hell" after death, but one remains in his astral body and increases his knowledge of the good, the true and the beautiful until he reaches the highest plane of consciousness where men and women like Jesus, Buddha and Socrates reside. Then one can travel anywhere in the Universe. I now believe that what I seek is the freedom of my astral body . . . a person can gain control of his subconscious mind, his conscious mind and his superconscious mind . . . This control of the psychic powers of the Asians and their monistic viewpoint of life is the new kind of religion that is needed to enrich the Western humanist culture amid its crumbling religions.

December 13, 1968

You will recall that I mentioned a Tibetan who now lives in an Englishman's body since his astral body was joined to it. This man says . . .that the psychic adepts of India and Tibet often assume various sex postures in order to stimulate their psychic energy portions of the body. I myself have found that there is a direct connection between sexual energy and psychic energy. And I am convinced that it is due to this energy that we survive bodily death. I have had some success in leaving my body, and I may be able to appear to you in my astral body sometime in the near future.

Norman's increasingly severe inhibitions are apparent in his hope of what the evolutionary process will accomplish in man:

"It will get to the point where a man's body will not be

important. He will be sexless. There will be no elimination. His brain will overshadow everything."

In the meantime, as the following letter indicates, Norman strives for, indeed, claims a knowledge of, that condition which the rest of the race can only anticipate in future generations:

February 25, 1969

. . . In the first ages of the earth, certain organisms of the marine type had to survive in the atmosphere outside of water. To do this they developed a mechanism which converted oxygen to water and then to light. They thus gave off a glow like the firefly today does, but of a warmer type. Later, when these organisms developed a type of air lung, the mechanism was no longer needed, so *this* light was turned inward forming the spine, the nervous system, reactions to light, eyesight and finally consciousness. This "turning inward" of light is, I believe, the key to the development of the superconscious; and this is what psychedelic drugs do . . . When an intense erotic feeling comes upon me, instead of allowing an erection of my genitals, I completely relax that area and allow the nerves to make the forward and backward movement of my pelvic area—with the stress upon the *backward* movement instead of the forward movement. (It is the forward movement that activates an orgasm.) Thus the energy turns inward. My heart (which I imagine as a vagina) pumps on the forward stroke. I imagine the blood as a penis, and on the backward stroke it enters the heart. Then I begin to inhale on the forward stroke and exhale on the backward stroke. As I exhale I sound "om" (as in "home") with my larynx, while imagining the larynx as a vagina and the air and sound as a penis entering it. I then concentrate upon my pituitary gland. As I inhale, the pineal gland withdraws from my pituitary gland, and as I exhale it enters the pituitary. (I imagine the latter as a vagina and the former as a penis.) This is the marriage of the pineal and the pituitary, and the internal "orgasm" which occurs brings about a reproduction which is sometimes called "the third eye" . . . I have made my peace with my subconscious, and it has been wedded to my conscious. Out of this wedding is being born a personality that will shed the old one as the baby chick sheds its eggshell. This is a true baptism. . . Regarding astral travel, Boroaster holds that there are planes surrounding all heavenly bodies and that man evolves to a state where he can travel to the highest plane, which is what we call God. The astral plane is the lowest plane. Astral bodies are confined to this plane. As the person evolves, his astral body "dies" and he leaves for a higher plane in the body that was inside his astral body.

Given the history of pain and punishment which Norman has experienced with regard to his own and others' bodies—his mother's outrage at his sexual curiosity, his sister's embarrassment at his interest in her, his peers' derision at his lack of control, and society's horror at his sexual behaviors—the fact that Norman has turned his original preoccupation inside-out should come as no surprise.

Feminine Identification

DREAMS

One of the clearest sex differences in dream contents is the ratio of male to female characters. Male dreamers have many more male characters than female characters in their dreams, while women have about the same number of each sex in their dreams. The ratio of males to females in the dreams of American men is approximately 2 to 1. In the dreams of American women the ratio is 1 to 1, the same ratio which was found in Norman's dreams. On the basis of this piece of data one would suppose that Norman has a feminine identification. It must be remembered, however, that the bulk of the female characters which appear in Norman's dreams involve his mother and sister and that this may be more expressive of his dependency upon the nuclear family than of a crystallized cross-sex identification. Other evidence from Norman's dreams that at first glance would appear to indicate a feminine identification is no more conclusive. The fact that he has homosexual relations does not in itself signify femininity, particularly since he plays an active as well as a passive role in these relationships. The fact that in one of his dreams Norman cuts off his penis might indicate a desire to be transformed into a woman, but it could also represent the wish for self-punishment ("If the eye offends, pluck it out"). Even Norman's concern with interior space, congruent with a feminine orientation, may express a general preoccupation with internal processes and their products which may be associated primarily with Norman's fetal interest and imagery.

Probably of more significance are Norman's dreams of dressing in women's clothes, of having a protruding chest much like a woman's breast and of the thought that he would make a magnificent woman. Such dreams can be considered more certain evidence of Norman's movement in the direction of a cross-gender identification. It should also be noted that there is a low incidence of both weapons and recreational elements in Norman's dreams—object categories more characteristic of male dreams—which may suggest a feminine disposition on Norman's part. In addition, the incidence of physical aggression in Norman's dreams is much lower than that of the norm group, and more like the incidence found in female dreams.

There is some evidence, then, to support the conclusion that Norman does identify himself with femaleness, certainly to a stronger degree than the average male. And yet his female identification has a tentative quality about it, not at all like what is accomplished in the transsexual, or even in certain transvestites or homosexuals. Norman's female identification is hardly stronger than his male identification. He is still in the larval stage where sexual identity is yet to be realized.

> I walked through a yard to a street. I squatted down. A stout lady came, and noticing that I wore a dress with men's trousers underneath, looked at me contemptuously and asked me why I was dressed that way. I was surprised because I had not realized that I was still wearing the dress. I took it off . . . I passed some stores, and I stopped in one to put the dress away.

WAKING BEHAVIOR

The test materials and inventories indicate that Norman possesses many characteristics normally associated with females

and very few so-called "masculine" traits. From his Rorschach responses one would conclude that Norman avoids
competition and is lacking in self assertion. This coincides
with his own self-description; in the Bills Index of Adjustment and Values he describes himself as very seldom "competitive." Norman's high feminine score on the Minnesota
Multiphasic Personality Inventory (MMPI) would lead one to
characterize him as a relatively passive, imaginative, and
sensitive male who is apt to enter into a "feminine" engagement with the world around him. And again this description
agrees with his own. In recalling the way he generally saw
himself during the time he was growing up (until he reached
the age of eighteen), Norman indicated that he was more
inadequate than adequate, more weak than strong, more good
than bad, more pleasant than unpleasant, more sweet than
sour, more powerless than powerful, and more dependent
than independent. He saw himself as equally feminine *and*
masculine.

There are a number of factors which reflect and have contributed to the fairly large measure of "femininity" that is
found in his make-up. First, although he claims to have identified with certain aspects of both parents, apparently he has
identified no more with one parent than the other. He describes himself as "physically masculine and dignified like
my father and compassionate and artistic like my mother,"
but at the same time he reports that he did not really feel like
either parent:

"In my primary qualities I am not similar to either of them.
I do not have my mother's obsession for practicality nor my
father's cynicism which amounted to nihilism." Although his
mother was the dominant, and finally the exclusive, parent in
the household, Norman's identification with her was not particularly strong. If it had been stronger, then given the fact
that she displayed more "masculine" than "feminine" characteristics, probably Norman would have accomplished a
stronger "masculine" identification. Obviously Norman's
own confusion was determined, in part, by parental role
models whose behaviors and roles would have been found

more appropriately in the parent of the opposite sex. Norman's father was ineffectual, confused with regard to his own sex role, and generally weak and dependent upon Norman's mother whose criticisms and directions he resented. On the other hand, Norman's mother was the "phallic" parent, the most dominant and aggressive member of the household. Norman's responses to the projective and other materials indicate that he viewed her as insensitive and self-centered, controlling in her behavior toward him, strong, ambitious, competitive, busy, confident, purposeful, and dependable. A tomboy in her own childhood, disdainful of men generally, it was Norman's mother who ruled the family and not her husband. Her behaviors with regard to her husband and her attitudes towards him as a male were surely observed by and communicated to her son. The consequences of that example for Norman's own gender identification must have been considerable.

Second, Norman's confusion and disinclination to describe himself as male *or* female may be the result of his peculiar oedipal situation. Norman became inordinately close to both parents; he was able to assume the female role with his father (which will be discussed in detail later on) and the masculine role with his mother (on an emotional level at least he served as a husband-substitute for his mother). He was, then, neither required nor motivated to crystallize his sexual object choice by repressing certain of his libidinal interests and by identifying with one or the other parent.

Third, as already noted, Norman has lived a good deal of his life in an exclusively feminine environment. His father was often absent even before he was finally driven from the household. Of considerable interest is the fact that when asked about those persons whom he considered to have been of most positive significance in his life, Norman named his mother, his sister, his aunt, and only one male, a professor whom he has come to know. The persons whom he considered a negative influence on his life are all male: his father, a male relative, a clergyman, a male teacher, and a male professor.

Fourth, Norman never had a very close friend of the same sex. His interests and talents were different from those of his male peers. He was not emotionally prepared to cope with the usual stresses of male social relationships in childhood and adolescence. On the other hand, his relationships with members of the opposite sex were no less stressful. Such a situation would tend to increase Norman's gender ambivalence, to set up an avoidance–avoidance conflict which would impel him to leave the field when it came to any kind of firm gender commitment. That lack of commitment is reflected further in his responses to the Rorschach where he disregards the popular symbols of male genitalia and expresses a revulsion for female genitalia. In Card VI the phallic symbol is not included with the rest of the card. Forms usually associated with female genitalia are described as a butterfly (Card II) or as part of an insect (Card VI), but his usual imagery with regard to the female's secondary sex characteristics is imbued with different, distinctive negative qualities. He sees a head of a spear that is savage and crude (Card II), a skunk (Card VII) and, not unrelated perhaps to the last image, the tailfeathers and flesh of fowl (Card IV). Is it possible that there is a connection in Norman's mind between the word fowl, and the word, foul, suggesting a powerfully negative association with the female genitals?

Probably the least that can be said is that Norman's failure to achieve a masculine identification tends to give the impression that a cross-sex identification has occurred. That conclusion may not be justified. It may be that Norman has deliberately not progressed to that point in a person's psychosexual development where either a same-sex or a cross-sex identification becomes finalized.

Fetal Identification

DREAMS

Life begins in an enclosure, and the organism remains in that enclosure for nine months. It has been argued elsewhere (Hall, 1967) on the basis of evidence secured from dreams that this interior existence has a profound influence upon the individual's personality and behavior. In Norman's case, this influence seems to have been particularly marked.

It has already been noted that interior space is prominent in Norman's dreams, and that entering and leaving are common modes of his reactions to the environment. Holes through which he enters or leaves are frequent elements in his dreams. Tunnels and shafts which Norman traverses and caves which he visits are also common. There are also other features of his dream productions which may have a fetal origin. The adjective, narrow, is frequently applied to passageways, streets, rooms, and buildings. There are odd perceptions of slanting which may refer to his original environment. Vibrations and shaking sensations, reminiscent of fetal movements, are experienced by Norman in his dreams.

> I was in a department store. A chair was displayed; I saw that it was vibrating. When I touched it the floor began to vibrate too.

> I was in a house. A washing machine in the next room was vibrating so violently that it was shaking the whole house.

There are two other features to Norman's dreams which may refer to the fetal state. The first pertains to nudity. Norman is often unclothed or partially clothed in his dreams. While references to nakedness may refer to infancy as well as to prenatal life, it is more characteristic of the latter state. The second, and perhaps more outstanding, reference which Norman makes very frequently is to swimming.

> I was getting dressed to go swimming in a pool with my sister. I was annoyed because I kept forgetting to put on something.

> I knew of a swimming pool hidden underground. I used some levers to uncover the pool so I and the others with me could use it.

> I tried to swim in a pool with water three feet deep, but it was too shallow. A woman dressed like a nurse arose from a chair, spread-

ing her legs as she arose. She said that if I paid admission I eould use the large pool on the other side of the glass wall. I paid her, but when I came to the pool I found that it was covered with a granite floor.

I wanted to go swimming. I went through an entrance, but I did not get an opportunity to swim.

Swimming is probably Norman's favorite recreational activity. It is mentioned very often in his dreams, and almost to the exclusion of any other form of recreation. More important, being immersed in water is directly analogous to the immersion of the fetus in uterine liquid. Some have considered swimming symbolic of a regression to prenatal existence. Evidence of this is provided further in the fetal imagery of Norman's other dreams which becomes increasingly direct:

I was aboard a large liner. The rooms were like hospital rooms. The doors also were like hospital doors. The ship suddenly began to sway.

There was a building and a swimming pool in the courtyard. Flowers were growing.

I was in a place with other people. There was a toilet bowl that was about four feet deep to the bottom. Some towels were down there. I flushed the toilet, and they moved. I tried to reach them. I reached one, and I put it where it belonged. I could see the other towels, but I could not reach them. (Yesterday I read that dreaming of flushing a toilet symbolized the embryo's attempt to flush out of the womb the unwanted fetus that had been stillborn before its conception.)

I was swimming in a pool. I made large bubbles by clapping my hands in the water. One was big enough for me to get inside. It felt like plastic. I prepared to get inside the bubble.

All of this evidence implies that Norman's infantile character extends back into the womb. His is not only a pregenital character; it is also prenatal.

WAKING BEHAVIOR

It is difficult to get any direct evidence for the extent to which Norman may be attracted to the uterine environment. There is a great deal, however, about Norman's style of life in the past and at the present time which may express an insistence on staying put, a determination to withdraw from the world around him into a womb-like existence. It has already been observed that Norman has never, of his own volition, strayed very far from home-base. When he was drafted and went overseas, his mother engineered a discharge. The reports from two institutions where he had been hospitalized during psychotic episodes indicate that he was released to his mother's custody at her insistence and against medical advice. And there he has remained in the drab and colorless environment of his mother's household. This is where he feels relatively secure, just as he did in the institutions where he had been confined for so long. Even Norman's work in a printing plant may be construed, in part, as being womb-oriented. And his one favorite recreational activity, swimming, may be considered similarly. It may be a mistake, however, to seek evidence for Norman's fetal identification in one or another isolated fact about his waking life. It is when his way of life—his central preoccupations, his usual engagements with the world, his perceptions of himself and others—is considered in its entirety that one can sense the extent to which Norman may consider his expulsion from his mother's womb with terror and profound regret.

Externalized Superego

DREAMS

During development, a child typically passes from a period when moral sanctions and prohibitions are imposed by external authorities to a period when moral standards become internalized, and feelings of pride and guilt act as self-regulators of conduct. One can speak of an internalized superego during the second period. Norman's dreams indicate that he is still in the first period of an externalized superego.

Feces kept coming out of my mouth. I couldn't stop it, and I was afraid I would have to choke before I could stop. The feces seemed to symbolize the indictment held against me for the crime I had committed. It seemed to be telling me that the only way I'd get the indictment disposed of and vindicate myself would be to do something drastic like choking.

I was talking with a man whom I at first mistook for a doctor, but later saw was a judge. He was trying my case. I told him I was sorry about committing the offense.

I was walking in a place that looked like a stadium. A man who looked like the charge officer on my former ward came over to me and said he would help me. He said, "You know that it is a serious thing to molest a child, don't you?" I said, "Yes, I do."

I was home from the hospital. I begged a lawman to let me stay free. I said that I would avoid children altogether.

I was among some girls about ten years old. I was tempted to touch them sexually. A plastic balloon shaped like a crotch was by me, and I felt it. I was dismayed because I had been tempted. I wanted to convince the doctors at the hospital where I was confined that I could control myself if they released me. I said to a doctor, "Is that why you won't let me go?" I pondered deeply on how I could rechannel my mental energy toward creative endeavors.

I was wandering through the streets. I saw a girl about 8, but I did not approach her, because I was afraid I would get into trouble.

There are a number of references in Norman's dreams to shame over molesting children or even over the thought of doing so. He appears to feel proud of himself when he does not yield to temptation and to be conscience stricken sometimes when he acts upon the impulse. On these occasions, however, his shame or guilt does not seem to be very sincere. Even his professed religious sentiments do not seem to go very deep. Norman appears, in fact, to have no very coherent set of values. His moral conflicts proceed largely from fears of being apprehended. He is afraid of being caught, not by an internalized superego, but by external authorities.

> I awoke to find I had been sleeping next to a dead man. I went to another part of the house, and when I returned the body was gone ... I was worried that I would get into trouble with the police if the body was found. I had recently gotten into trouble with the police.

> I was on the ledge of a snow covered cliff. Policemen were looking for a criminal. They saw me just as I was pulling up my trousers. I was embarrassed.

Norman's guilt is very shallow. Embarrassment is his most common reaction, a superficial and transient emotion compared to either shame or guilt. He never seems to be tortured by his misdeeds, although he makes a show of feeling ashamed. He is moralistic rather than moral, and his professions of religious feelings are rhetorical rather than real. Even his desires not to be caught are somewhat hypocritical since he does get caught and even, it may be supposed, wants to be.

In conclusion, Norman has a young child's superego and not that of an adult, which is to say that his personality is tainted by psychopathy.

WAKING BEHAVIOR

Norman's mental abilities are organized fairly efficiently, and he is capable of superior intellectual achievement. Tests administered to him in 1960 and again in 1967 indicate this most clearly. Although Norman left school before graduation at the insistence of a mother who could see no value in an education, his academic performance had been above average. Later he was able to finish high school by correspondence, and he is presently enrolled full-time as a college student. During the time that he was growing up he was deeply religious and attended church at least twice a week. While he was attending parochial school he recalls a deep conflict regarding religion; he could not decide if he should believe or not. Admittedly his religious involvement has consisted chiefly of raising intellectual or philosophical questions, and yet at least on this level he appears to have grappled with moral issues as well.

Given Norman's background as well as his mental capacities, how is it that he could have repeatedly committed the criminal offenses which led to incarcerations in six different institutions? Certainly this is one of the principal questions which must be raised by the present study. Were Norman's antisocial acts a function of his mental state or a reflection of his character? Was Norman so out of touch with reality that he did not know what he was doing, or did he know what he was doing and did not care or could not help himself? If the latter is true then one would have to conclude that Norman is, to use an older term, simply morally defective, that his internal controls are not sufficiently well developed to be effective, that his superego is externalized, that is, he depends upon external restraints for acting in socially approved ways. If this is the case, then he will probably have to remain in a highly structured environment in order to stay out of trouble. On the other hand, if Norman was psychotic ("crazy") at the times that he committed his anti-social acts, then as long as his psychosis remains in a state of remission, it will be possible for him to remain outside of an institution and continue to function in socially acceptable ways.

In 1945, and at the age of seventeen, after sexual advances to a teenage girl in a public park, Norman was admitted to a municipal mental institution by order of the city court. He was found to be ignorant of social relationships and received the diagnosis of "simple adult maladjustment." Four years later, he was admitted to a state mental hospital and found to be out of contact, apathetic, withdrawn, uncooperative, and mute. He had both visual and auditory hallucinations in which he was made to feel guilty. At that time he received twenty-six shock treatments, and although his condition improved, he soon became negativistic again and showed signs of a catatonic stupor. He was released on convalescent status within six months and discharged a year later with a diagnosis of Dementia Praecox: Catatonic Type, Condition: recovered. Five months later Norman was admitted to a different state hospital where he remained three months. During that time he denied hallucinations, did not believe that his interest in talking with children was strange, and his affect appeared shallow. He was placed on convalescent care with a diagnosis of Dementia Praecox; Hebephrenic Type, and discharged one year later. His next admission to another mental institution occurred eight years later (in 1959) and at the age of thirty-one, at which time a diagnosis of Schizophrenia: Mixed Type was made. He was found to be withdrawn, suspicious, and his affect was flattened although he was well oriented. Seven months later he was transferred to a veterans hospital, where although delusions and hallucinations were denied, his judgment and insight was found to be poor. Two months later Norman was taken to the county jail and then committed to a state hospital for the criminally insane. At the time of his commitment Norman appeared perplexed. He was apathetic and apprehensive, and his affect was extremely flattened. His orientation and memory were good, but his retention and immediate recall were grossly impaired. There was no gross delusional ideation and no paranoid symptomatology. Of some interest to our present consideration of Norman is the diagnostic statement which was made after his admission (in 1960) to this particular hospital:

"The diagnosis in this case could be considered as Psychosis with Psychopathic Personality with Abnormal Sexuality, when looking superficially at this case. However it appears that there are basically in this man manifestations which indicate a more malignant process, characterized by withdrawal, autism, and inappropriate affect although no pronounced delusions are present, and hallucinations were only temporary several years ago. Therefore, the writer feels that a diagnosis of Schizophrenia; Undifferentiated Type is justified."

Five years later (and two years after Norman had begun to

record his dreams) Norman was discharged from the hospital. At that time the history of his stay in the hospital was reviewed:

"On admission to this hospital, the patient showed symptoms of a malignant functional mental disease. Concerning his alleged criminal offense, he knew his charges but used the mental mechanism of projection, blaming his parents for his misdeeds. Eventually the patient gained insight into his alleged criminal offense. At a recent presentation to our special release committee, the patient was able to give a coherent and relevant account of the events leading to his arrest for the alleged criminal offense."

Norman was discharged and returned to the court to face his charges. After a series of legal maneuvers, Norman was returned to another state hospital and then transferred once again to the veterans hospital where the tests of the present study were administered. Again, evidence of a schizoid personality was found in the Minnesota Multiphasic Personality Inventory (MMPI). Some experts would maintain that his MMPI profile (see Appendix II) indicates an established schizophrenic process. At the very least it is suggestive of a severe and alienated character disorder. And if, as some suppose, scoring high on the paranoia and schizophrenia scales — regardless of the configuration of the MMPI profile as a whole — is a strong indication of paranoid schizophrenia, then it would appear that Norman is attempting to maintain an equilibrium in ways that are *not* primarily psychopathic in tone and quality.

There is other evidence that would tend to refute the notion that Norman is a sociopath. A review of his life reveals guilt over masturbation, guilt over the sexual experiences he had with his father, and already noted, guilt over his desire to explore the body of a female playmate. Prior to Norman's second commitment to a hospital, he kept saying: "It was my fault . . . a big sinner . . . a dirty boy." His hallucinations were self-accusatory. In the Incomplete Sentences (see Appendix II) he writes: "*My greatest fear* is just punishment; *I am very* attracted to pleasure but it does not make me happy; *My greatest worry* is evil, how 'to recognize it and what to do about it." Such expressions are not usually made by a sociopath. Most sociopaths present a picture of unbridled impulsivity without a twinge of regret—many hardened criminals present such a picture—and although Norman has committed numerous offenses, this in itself cannot be taken as evidence of psychopathy. It is possible that, regardless of their unconscious motivations, Norman's activities were, in his own mind at least, more platonic than erotic, more expressive of an intellectual curiosity than of a wanton sensuality. Until the last incident—and he has not molested a child since—it was possible for him to maintain that he never harmed his victims. The great majority of the children Norman came into contact with were never even aware of his intentions or of his erotic responses. He approached and left them in a friendly fashion, with no one the wiser. To be sure, Norman gave evidence of little ego strength in the pursuit of activities which were extraordinarily self-destructive. He did not take social reality into account and suffered the consequences. And yet, given his emotionally impoverished home life, on another level perhaps it was a removal from his familial environment which he actually sought.

Finally, it is possible to argue that because Norman experienced excessive guilt, was *superego-ridden*, he came to renounce all feeling, to overly control his emotions, and thus to give the impression that his experience of shame over his anti-social behaviors was superficial.

In a psychological report given in 1960 Norman is described as possessing "a personality rigidly defended by obsessive-compulsive mechanisms." The same was true of him in 1967. It appears that Norman clings desperately to obsessive-compulsive defenses as his only basis for hope that he might yet survive the dreaded onslaught from within. His responses to the Rorschach indicate a compulsive meticulousness, intellectualization and compulsion, over-ideation, a pedantic emphasis upon and need for accuracy, a powerful rigidity, and an extensive constriction. His responses to the other tests show an overuse of whatever intellectual talents he possesses, an inflexibility, a ruminative self-doubt, and extreme obsessionalism. Norman's test scores and reponses leave little doubt as to the nature and pervasiveness of the defenses which he uses to contain the anxiety which threatens to break through. He is intent that every aspect of his life be stripped bare of all emotional and affectional nuances. Were he to depart from this intent he is fearful that he would lose his bearings.

From Norman's responses to the Rorschach one would have to conclude that he represses any tendency to act in accordance with his own emotional reactions. His is a self-imposed impotence which requires the removal of teeth from alligators and horns from a ferocious moose. He disavows, in his undue inhibition of any impulse, the sexual and aggressive elements of his own personhood. Such defenses serve to lower the level of his drive and activity, to substantially reduce whatever energy Norman may have for acting out, and they account for his less harmful apathy and listlessness. Among other things, however, a price is paid in the unavailability of productive energies to back up his intellectual interests and ambitions. Anyone meeting Norman in 1967 would not have found it difficult to believe that for a period of time he lived in a catatonic stupor.

Some of the test data suggest that Norman's is only an apparent, surface apathy, that his colossal self-control, his measured physical and vocal gestures, are due to an unevenly renounced impulsivity, to a deep-seated conflict between what he seeks and what he displays. The strength of that conflict is alluded to in some of his Thematic Apperception Test imagery: in the man about to embark upon some kind of criminal activity from which he cannot be dissuaded, in the young man who, lacking moral courage, will avenge himself. Norman walks unsteadily a narrow line between the stultification of self-control and the anarchy of self-expression. Now and then he senses the enormity of his repressive maneuvers, of the defenses which he musters in behalf of his personal and social survival. His temptation to do things that are considered unconventional, to avoid situations in which others expect him to conform still remains.

Of special relevance to this topic is Norman's memory of what took place when he was arrested in 1959. He told the officer that the officer's conscience would bother him if he arrested him. The officer replied, "You have no conscience." Norman's following comments may go further in revealing his apparent lack of conscience than anything that has been pointed out so far in this discussion:

"As I reflected on this incident later, I recalled my past, and the *irony* of his words pierced me; the years of guilt, because I did not tell my mother about my father's 'sinful' behavior, that climaxed in my nervous breakdown and commitment to the hospital where I was condemned for eternity to hell because of my part in my father's 'sin.' If I had no conscience I surely would not have sentenced myself to eternal hell. Yet, perhaps the officer was right. Perhaps life had become so unreal that my own conscience had become unreal to me."

FOUR

**Dreams and Personality:
Additional Observations**

What are some of the reasons that Norman has a polymorphously perverse infantile character? The explanations, like the previous description of his personality, come first from an independent analysis of Norman's dreams and then from information provided by the other sources.

What must first be decided is whether Norman has always had an infantile character (fixation) or whether he regressed to it during his adult life as a result of a traumatic experience. This is a matter of some importance since if it is regressive it would be easier for Norman to overcome than if it is a fixation. On the basis of his dreams one would have to conclude that Norman has never grown up emotionally, that on this level he has always been a child.

If this is true, then what prevented Norman from growing up? One obvious explanation is that his mother, who appears so frequently in his dreams, overprotected him to such an extent that he was unable to form relationships with his peers and to identify with males. Norman's mother may have wanted to keep him an asexual, undifferentiated infant who would always be dependent upon her. She herself was probably hostile towards males, and this would tend to arouse conflicts in Norman regarding his own masculinity. He grew up in an exclusively female environment consisting of his mother, sister, and aunt, yet Norman's dreams provide additional data which suggest that an overprotective mother and an exclusively female environment were not the principal determinants of his infantile character. And it is to these data that we must now turn.

Relation to His Father

DREAMS

The fact that Norman's dreams include not one direct reference to his father is amazing. The complete absence of the father suggests that Norman never knew him or that any memories of him have been so severely repressed that they do not appear even in his dreams. Fortunately, there are a few dreams in which a father appears.

> There was a man, a woman and a boy nearby. The boy was their son. The wife and son said they were leaving because of something he did. They went down a stairs to the basement of a building. The boy wanted to do something drastic, but the mother held him back. Then she told him to bury a bundle of sticks that she handed him in the basement. The boy took it and went downstairs.

Norman's association (one of the few he records in his dream diary) to the bundle of sticks is "faggot," a slang expression for a certain type of homosexual. He says of this association, "It seems to be related to my relations with my father." Was Norman's father bisexual? Did he ever use his son sexually? This possibility is suggested by a dream in which a bull tried to have sexual relations with Norman. In psychoanalytic totem theory, totem animals stand for tribal fathers (ancestors). If such is the case, then in Norman's dreams, his father is represented by strong, dangerous animals such as a bear, dragon, elephant, bucking horse, and fox.

These dreams suggest that Norman considers his father to be a dangerously impulsive person. If that impulsivity was expressed sexually, was this the reason why the father left or was required to leave the family? Was his behavior considered so disgraceful that any memory of him was blotted out of the family, and therefore out of Norman's dreams?

> Someone was coming to harm me. I saw his figure as I lay on a bed. I tried to call my mother who was in the house, but I could not pronounce the words. I could only make a sound. My jaw froze open.

Freud (1905) has written concerning the polymorphously perverse disposition:

> It is an instructive fact that under the influence of seduction children can become polymorphously perverse, and can be led into all possible kinds of sexual irregularities. This shows that an aptitude for them is innately present in their disposition. There is consequently little resistance towards carrying them out, since the mental dams against sexual excesses — shame, disgust, and morality — have either not yet been constructed at all or are only in the course of construction, according to the age of the child.

Was Norman actually seduced by his father or was it an imaginary seduction? If such paternal behavior occurred, was it sufficiently traumatic to freeze the son's personality development? It is difficult to say. Doubtless, something pertaining to the father was traumatic for the son. The necessary, if not sufficient, condition for Norman's child complex would appear to be his relationship with his father which may be viewed in still another way.

> I was the son of a knight. Suddenly, about ten ornamental balls topped with birds fell from the balcony I was on. A woman came and said that because of that accident my father would lose his knighthood. I was angry. I said, "Woman, I will see that you don't take away his knighthood. I have something to say about that."

In this dream, a fantasied father is depicted as a noble and manly person. The elevated rank of the fantasied father is probably in sharp contrast with the actual father's position in society.

The more important dynamic significance of the dream, however, is to be found in the two symbolic castration themes: 1) the falling of the bird-topped balls, and 2) the threatened loss of the father's knighthood. Moreover, the boy's symbolic castration is made the *cause* of the father's threatened castration. This may be a reversal of cause and effect. It is possible that Norman's conception of his father's castration causes Norman to feel castrated. Note also that it is a woman who is seen as the castrator. Norman appears to be defending his father against a mother figure. Does this dream, then, denote Norman's identification with a castrated father?

The choice of the word knighthood is possibly not without symbolic significance. As Thass-Thienemann has shown, the suffix hood which is appended to so many English words has an etymological relation to foreskin. Moreover, knight belongs to a linguistic complex of words which includes knave, king, kind, knee, and know, whose basic Latin root word means to beget. The loss of one's knighthood as a castration metaphor is supported by etymology.

It may be hypothesized that Norman, lacking a father and growing up in an entirely female interpersonal environment, had no opportunity to form an identification with a male. This would create a grave problem of gender identity. It would also serve to impair Norman's superego development and tend to fixate him in the pregenital stage.

WAKING BEHAVIOR

For as long as he could remember, Norman had viewed his father as "a complete failure as a father, husband, and wage earner." Norman's descriptive adjectives of his father include: inadequate, cold, unsuccessful, absent, unpleasant and unprotective. In the relationship he had with his son he was hostile, rejecting, and harsh. Even if this were all that was known about him and the father-son relationship, one would have predicted many difficulties for Norman in his attempt to move through the normal course of psychosexual development. But when one considers the even more unusual and potentially traumatic aspects of that relationship in the evidence which follows, there can be no doubt about the central importance of Norman's relationship with his father in determining Norman's subsequent psychological and interpersonal difficulties.

When Norman was four years old, his father forced him to suck his penis:

"I felt bewildered. The size of his erection frightened me. I had never been approached like that before by my father. In fact, I can't recall ever having had sexual thoughts prior to that time. All I can remember is my father's hypnotic, angry stare as I tried to push his penis away from my face. It depicted vengeance, retribution, destruction. The memory of that stare is vivid and was reinforced by subsequent ones. I feared for my life. I felt drawn by my father's almost hypnotic force."

This experience was relived in a dream he had, perhaps more than once, in late adolescence:

"I was a young boy, four years old. The room, the carpet were all familiar. My father was there. Something happened before the climax, but it's difficult to remember. My father was walking toward me, staring like a hypnotist. I was frightened that if I backed up I'd fall off the edge or something. I woke up on the floor next to the bed."

According to one of the hospital reports, this incestuous activity—Norman's sucking of his father's penis—continued until his father left the family. The report also suggests that although Norman was traumatized by the initial experience, he came to enjoy this unusual attention from his father. Norman's latest report, made at the time of this present investigation, indicates his strong ambivalence:

"During the early years, I tried desperately to decide what to do about my father's actions with me. I decided to do nothing, and I never did decide whether I was doing the right thing by doing nothing or whether I was sinning. I often had spells in which the feeling that I was being exploited was mingled with a feeling that I wanted to be exploited, and in the midst of these feelings came the feeling of erotic ecstasy, mingled with a feeling that I was taking something that I did not deserve to have. I then would pound my pillow in anguish at being involved in this human situation, and rage against the human condition that was manifested by my inability to cope with it and grasp the meaning of my father's behavior."

Later, in the same paragraph which deals primarily with Norman's religious feelings, he draws the analogy, "I felt like a maiden being ravished but I welcomed it."

The depth and exact details of Norman's feelings about his father and their relationship will never be known. Too much has been repressed. The Thematic Apperception Test material indicates that Norman either disregards the father's presence entirely or else the "older man" is described as morally depraved and associated with an early traumatic experience which had a profound effect upon the hero's subsequent development:

"The incident will affect him (the boy, later referred to as the man's son) throughout his lifetime, his judgements and decisions, and his relationships with other people. He will present an apathetic front toward other people, but this is only on the surface; underneath there is tender feeling."

If the seduction and subsequent sexual activities actually occurred—and Norman's insistence over the years during both the psychotic and non-psychotic periods of his life that they did occur, as well as his mother's memory of Norman's strange behavior and listlessness at the time Norman claims the seduction took place makes the investigators believe that the incidents were not merely fantasies—the consequences would have been monumental. Norman was ill-prepared for what his father required of him. Norman could not be expected to cope very successfully with the feelings which were surely evoked. The secret which Norman carried for the first twenty-two years of his life must have created a grave distortion in his mind with regard to his place in the world and to the meaning and consequences of sociosexual encounters in general.

Addendum

The following questions, seven in all, were formulated by Bell after he had read Hall's report which was based upon the dream material. They were sent to Hall whose answers were given before he knew anything about Norman aside from what he learned from his dreams.

1a. How would you describe Norman's interpersonal relationships?

1b. How would you describe the kind of relationship Norman had with his sister in childhood and/or their mutual relationship with each parent?

There are only two persons with whom Norman seems to have any sort of a continuing, meaningful relationship: his mother and his sister. He is very close to his sister, and they have probably always been close. They seem to form a union against the world, and sometimes against the mother. Since the father does not come into Norman's dreams, it is difficult to say how Norman or his sister reacted to the father, although some inferences have been made in answering Question 3.

Norman has no relationships with known peer females, and his relationships with known peer males are limited to interactions with other inmates. He is not especially close to any of the other inmates, although he does have intellectual discussions with one or two of them, and there is some sexual activity which is not accompanied by an affective relationship.

Norman's relations with his mother and with his sister consists of more friendly than aggressive interactions. In the case of the mother, she is more likely to befriend him: in the case of the sister, he is more likely to befriend her. It appears from the dreams, that Norman plays the same protective role toward his sister that his mother plays toward him.

Norman has no friendly or aggressive interactions with known females, but then there are only a handful of such characters in his dreams. With respect to known males, he has more friendly interactions than aggressive ones. He is more likely to be befriended by them than to be the befriender.

He has more friendly than aggressive interactions with unknown adult females, and more aggressive than friendly interactions with unknown adult males. In his aggressive interactions with unknown males and females, he is more often the victim than the aggressor. In his friendly encounters, the incidence of Norman as befriender and Norman as befriended is about equal.

He has many more friendly than aggressive interactions with minor females and about an equal number of friendly and aggressive interactions with minor males. In these encounters, Norman is aggressor and victim, and befriender and befriended about the same number of times.

In general, he has more friendly than aggressive relations with all classes of characters except for unknown adult males. The male stranger in dreams often symbolizes the father or an authority figure (Hall, 1963).

Norman's interpersonal relationships are very shallow and transient except for those with his mother and sister. Even when he is involved in an aggressive interaction, the aggression is weak rather than strong. Aside from his mother and sister, he had no viable or vital cathexes.

2. How would you describe his peer relationships in childhood and adolescence?

Norman had few if any meaningful peer relationships as a child or adolescent. He was a loner, except for his strong involvement with his mother and sister. There are few mentions in his dreams of boyhood friends or acquaintances. There is a suggestion in one dream that he may have had a traumatic or sexual experience with boyhood playmates.

Norman's sexual attraction to minors of both sexes may represent an attempt to compensate for his loneliness as a child. There is a suggestion in the dreams that his family may have moved often while he was growing up, so that he had little chance to establish permanent friendships. He may also use the childhood relationship with his sister as a model for his adult reactions to children.

3. Is there any evidence of apparently inconsistent perceptions of the father? If so, what are they?

Since Norman's father does not appear in any of the dreams, it will have to be inferred what his perceptions of his father are from symbols of the father.

The male adult stranger often stands for the father. The incidence of aggressive interactions between Norman and male strangers is higher than the incidence of friendly interactions. He has 116 aggressive encounters and 78 friendly encounters with male strangers. By comparison he has 37 aggressive and 57 friendly encounters with adult female strangers, and 18 aggressive and 36 friendly encounters with adult known males. In a large majority of the aggressive interactions with male strangers Norman is the victim of aggression. If male stranger is translated into father, then Norman perceives his father as being more hostile than nurturant toward him. This, however, is typical of male dreamers.

There are the usual Oedipal dreams in which Norman is competing with another man for the affection of a woman. But there are also dreams in which he defends a father-surrogate against a mother-surrogate. In one dream, he is sexually attracted to a father-figure; in another, a father-figure expresses paternal feelings toward Norman, and in another, he wants to go on a trip with an older man.

One dream suggests that the father may have committed suicide; another that he is dead. Another dream implies that Norman's sister was the father's favorite.

4. What would you guess his principal defense mechanism(s) to be?

Dreams are not very good at revealing defenses. They are, of course, themselves projections but this does not differentiate among dreamers.

There is a lot of regression in Norman's dreams, but as was argued previously, he is fixated at an early stage of psychosexual development, so it is not so much regression as it is fixation. One might, however, see him in waking life as engaging in a lot of regressive (fixated) behavior.

Norman is an intellectualizer. He seems to be interested in abstract ideas and reading philosophical and scientific books. And we know he is interested in writing. Some of this information comes not from dreams but from Norman's comments upon the dreams.

His defenses in waking life are not very effective, in any case; they do not keep him out of trouble.

5. *What is indicated regarding masturbation as a sexual outlet for Norman? What might be his views and practices in regard to this?*

Norman is a masturbator, and probably a chronic one. Anyone who fantasizes about sex as much as he does is almost certain to indulge in frequent masturbation. However, he tries to resist masturbating and to control himself, but the control is not very effective. He thinks of his body as being pure, clean and healthy when he refrains from having an orgasm.

It is interesting to see how sex and religion are associated in Norman's mind. Sex is an animal appetite, and religion as represented by the church (Catholic), his aunt (a nun), the Pope, and God, is clean, pure, and spiritual. Religion does not help him very much to control his impulses, probably because the Catholic Church provides an external superego (confession, communion, rituals, and images) which makes it unnecessary to internalize the conscience.

6. *What parts of the female anatomy would have the most erotic potential for Norman?*

In his dreams, Norman is polymorphously perverse not only with respect to the choice of a sexual partner, but he also tends to be versatile with respect to the parts of the body that excite him sexually. Genitals, breasts, buttocks, hips, legs, and hair all stimulate him. There is one region of the body, however, that takes precedence over the others, and that is the buttocks, and in others it is implied by such statements as being hugged or embraced from behind. It is not only the buttocks of another person that stimulates him, but his own as well. Nor does it make any difference whether it is the buttocks of a female or a male; they are both sexually arousing. This preference fits in whith his anal orientation.

Some psychoanalysts have equated the buttocks with the breasts, which may be an overdetermining factor in Norman's preference for the buttocks. He is not, however, primarily preoccupied with breasts although he gives some indication in his dreams that he would like to have breasts. But this is part of his wanting to be a woman. It may be observed that the penis is a much better breast symbol because it gives "milk" when sucked. Norman does not seem to be very much interested in sucking penises, although he probably likes to have his sucked which indicates a female identification.

7. Is there any evidence regarding the nature of Norman's molesting behavior?

Norman likes to have his penis held or sucked, to have children sit on his lap and fondle them, and to put his hand on various parts of their bodies. He often meets the children he molests on the street, and tries to entice them into the bushes. He sometimes offers them money. He is not aggressive or sadistic; on the contrary, he is usually gentle in his approach. He has misgivings about approaching children, whether out of fear of being apprehended and arrested or for some other reason, and he tries to control himself. He fantasizes about sex with children more than he actually performs it. He does not seem to be an exhibitionist with children.

Norman loves children. He wants to be companionable with them. He feels paternal or maternal toward them, and he has compassion for them. He is able to empathize with their problems. Norman plays the role of the nurturant yet seductive mother, which may be the way in which his mother treated him when he was a child.

Summary

DREAMS

The contents of Norman's dreams, either in themselves or when compared with the dreams of the norm group, provide a great deal of information pertaining to his personality and waking behaviors. They also suggest some of the reasons that Norman has become the person he is. What follows is based entirely on the dream analysis. It must be remembered that other than the age and gender of the dreamer, no other information was provided.

The most outstanding feature of Norman's personality is his extraordinary emotional immaturity. On every level of his existence, he remains a child. His infantile status is reflected in a polymorphously perverse disposition which fails to distinguish between one sexual object and another or one sexual act and another. Although Norman's sexual interests include a wide range of objects—male and female, child and adult—most of his sexual feelings are not acted out. In fact he is less active sexually than most males his age. Norman is probably a chronic masturbator, but even in this regard he tries to control himself to an unusual degree. Breasts, hips, legs, and hair excite him sexually, but it is the buttocks of both males and females which have the greatest erotic potential for Norman. He tends to be ambivalent towards female gentials. Another reflection of Norman's child-like personality is his unusual dependence upon his mother and sister for his emotional security. This dependency is of long-standing. During his childhood, possibly because his mother encouraged it or because his family did not stay in one place for any length of time, Norman had few friendships. Then, as now, Norman invested little of himself in others with whom he remained only superficially friendly. Another reason that Norman was and remains a "loner" is that his associations with other children were very painful. In fact it is reasonable to suppose that Norman's sexual activities with children represent, in part, the effort to make up for his original experience of loneliness in childhood. At that time Norman was forced to retreat to the nuclear family where he enjoyed a particularly close relationship with his sister (who was his father's favorite) whom he tended to protect in much the same way as his mother did with him. One aspect of their "union against the world" possibly included an explicitly sexual relationship which may have served as a model for his subsequent child "molestations." The fact that Norman was raised in an exclusive female environment and that his mother was probably hostile toward males in general probably accounts for the considerable confusion which Norman displays with regard to his own gender identity. He tends to reject any firm gender allegiance — he is no more male than female — and the fact that he is noncommital in this regard can be considered further evidence of Norman's infantile fixation. His ambiguous gender identification, expressed in certain fantasies about being a woman and in occasional instances of cross-sex dressing, may also be the result of a paternal relationship which made it impossible for Norman to identify with a male role model. His father, now dead, and possibly the result of suicide, was probably absent during much of Norman's childhood, or else there was something about his relationship with Norman that was so traumatic that Norman has entirely repressed it. It is possible that Norman's father used him sexually, and that this is the reason he was banished from the family and from the family's memory. Perhaps this is why Norman perceives the father as powerful, dangerous, and impulsive. On the other hand, there is evidence that Norman has identified with an ineffectual, "castrated" father. In either case, it would appear that Norman's distorted relationship with his father was the crucial determinant of Norman's renunciation of adulthood. The latter is most evident in Norman's inability to postpone certain gratifications, most notably those associated with his eliminative functions. In his childhood, and perhaps even at the present time, Norman was a chronic bedwetter. This lack of control over urination, and defecation as well, indicative of a strong expulsive mode in his psychological make-up, probably means that Norman is not able to save money, to keep a job, or to lead an orderly life. This lack of control is accompanied by an externalized superego. When Norman's defenses (primarily intellectualization) fail — which they usually do, accounting for his · frequent incarcerations — he experiences little guilt or shame. He is either embarrassed by his misdeeds or else annoyed by the inconvenience of hospitalization. He is not apt to see much wrong with having his penis sucked or held by little children or with seating children on his lap and fondling various parts of their bodies. Although he tries to control his pedophilic interests and behaviors, in this as in other matters, his attempts at self-control are unsuccessful. He has sought children out, not in aggressive or sadistic ways, but with an affection which may be reminiscent of the relationship he had with a highly nurturant but seductive mother.

WAKING BEHAVIOR

The data provided by personal conversations and correspondence with Norman, by psychological tests administered over a seven year period, and by records from the six different hospitals to which Norman had been committed, present the following picture.

Norman has failed to grow up in any real sense. He has been extremely dependent upon his mother throughout the course of his life, and he has come to rely upon her concern for him in very fundamental ways. In that as in other relationships he is more childlike than adult, and Norman's style of life indicates that he has sought to preserve an almost womblike existence. In keeping with his infantile status, there is some confusion with regard to his gender identification. He seems to have renounced masculine traits in himself, but at the same time he has not made a true feminine identification either. This gender ambivalence is probably the result of many factors. It was his mother who assumed the male functions in the household. He could not identify with his father whose extraordinary sexual relationship with his son further enhanced Norman's gender confusion. A principal result of these incestuous encounters was that Norman suffered an identity crisis from which he has never recovered. Other reasons for Norman's lack of a strong masculine identification include his having been raised in a female-dominated environment and his isolation from same-sex peers.

Another chief inpression of Norman which is gained from these particular data is that of his attempts to control his bodily impulses. He is less active sexually than other males his age, and all that is unusual about his sexual interests and sexual expression is their infantile quality: in the past, at least, most of his sexual arousal has occurred in the company of children and in connection with primarily voyeuristic behaviors. These activities can best be understood as the expression of an inadequate, infantile personality. At the time that they took place Norman was not experiencing a psychotic episode, and, on the other hand, his molestations were accompanied by feelings not usually found in the sociopath. They were probably more a continuation of his childhood preoccupations and conducted from a child's point of view. On one occasion in which Norman's behaviors amounted to more than this, he was so appalled that he sought an extraordinary self-control which would guarantee that such a thing would not happen again. It is this determination, reflected in Norman's intellectualization and obsessive-compulsive defenses, which is most clearly evident in the data derived from his waking behaviors.

FIVE

Dreams and Personality: Their Relationship

There is considerable agreement with regard to the picture of Norman which emerges from his dreams and from the case material. Sometimes this agreement involves rather broad aspects of his personality, and sometimes it has to do with specific behaviors which are evident in both his dreams and his waking life. These areas of agreement are considered as well as the relationship between our common findings and those of other investigators. Finally, differences between the dream and other data either with respect to what they tend to emphasize or which involve actual disagreements are examined.

Areas of Agreement

Although the dream analysis indicates more strongly and precisely the primitive quality of Norman's psychic life, data from other sources confirm that chief finding and offer examples of Norman's infantile personality in his waking life. From his dreams it was concluded that Norman was extremely dependent upon his nuclear family, and especially his mother, for emotional support; that within the family, Norman acts nurturantly towards his sister in much the same way that his mother acts toward him; that Norman has never had any vital interpersonal involvements outside the home; that he was a loner in childhood during which time the relationships with his peers were most unpleasant; that as an adult he continues to be remote from his peers of the same or opposite sex; and that he has not married and has no children. The other data agree with these conclusions in every respect. In addition, they add little or nothing to the information provided by Norman's dreams. The dreams indicate a kind of fetal identification on Norman's part, an exceedingly primitive experience of himself and his environment which is suggested by the kinds of places in which he lives and works and even by his interest in swimming. Again, Norman's waking life approximates very closely what has been said about him on the basis of his dreams. The only recreational activity which Norman enjoys is swimming, and his style of life is analogous to a womb-like existence. The dreams also indicate Norman's ambivalent feelings about the security which he enjoys, feelings that are also reflected in his conversations and test responses.

On the basis of Norman's dreams it is believed that his extraordinary (sexual) relationships with children resulted from the fact that Norman is, psychologically, more like a child than an adult; that his relationships with children are more positive than his relationships with adults; and that in his exchanges with adults he is apt to act in a child-like passive role. The other data agree entirely with these impressions. Norman's waking life amounts to little more than a reiteration of his childhood. He prefers children both sexually and socially because they are less threatening to him than adults. In all of his psychological reports, Norman is described as basically infantile. Perhaps this is what accounts for Norman's gender confusion or ambivalence which is so clearly reflected in his dreams. They indicate his puzzlement over sex differences as well as a female identification which is more prominent than what is found in the average male.

From his dreams it was suggested that Norman had failed to make the usual same-sex identification, that he displayed more feminine than masculine characteristics (although not the degree that this is found among transsexuals), that he probably dressed in female clothing from time to time (but was not an habitual transvestite), and that the reasons for Norman's feminine interests and gender confusion might be found in his mother's hostility towards males in general and in either his mother's or sister's attempts to feminize him by dressing him as a girl during his childhood. In every respect but one (Norman was not dressed in girls' clothes as a child) the other data agree with these findings. In his waking life Norman was found to: 1) be baffled by the differences between males and females, 2) dress in female clothing for strategic purposes associated with his molestations, and 3) protest against the masculine role but at the same time not accept the feminine role entirely either.

Other evidence for Norman's infantile status which the dreams provided pertains to what has been termed his polymorphously perverse disposition. This was indicated in his dreams by the number and kind of different characters Norman became involved with sexually (more than one-third were minors) and by the different kinds of sexual acts in which Norman appeared to be engaged. In this regard, however, it was pointed out that much of his sexuality was expressed more in fantasy than in actual behavior and that behaviorally he may be more controlled than the average male. This is certainly supported by the other data. Although Norman dreams of sexual encounters with his sister, in his waking life these remain only a fantasy or a repressed preoccupation. He dreams of sex with unfamiliar adult females, but has never had an orgasm with a woman. There are sexual dreams involving female adolescents, and yet Norman has made such sexual advances only once. His sexual dreams also include babies as sexual objects, and yet this experience does not appear in his sexual history. That history does, however, include sexual behaviors involving female children, male children, adolescents, and adults, and, on at least one occasion, an animal. And if the unfamiliar adult male or the bull in Norman's dreams is really Norman's father in disguise, then his sexual history, of course, includes that experience as well. The other data would agree with the conclusion that in his erotic fantasies and only in certain behaviors Norman can be considered polymorphously perverse. Unlike the dreams, the other data tend to emphasize the extent to which he seeks to *control* his sexual interests and behaviors. And while there is no evidence that Norman enjoys mouth-genital contacts (although he did come to enjoy these contacts with his father) or that he has ever engaged in this technique with children, there is evidence to support other matters suggested by his dreams: 1) the erotic potential which buttocks have for Norman, 2) his disinclination to act in sexually agressive or sadistic ways with children, and 3) his general although not complete lack of exhibitionistic tendencies.

Finally, there is remarkable agreement between the dreams and the other data with regard to Norman's father and their relationship. The absence of Norman's father in the dreams was interpreted as a function either of his father's absence or of their traumatic relationship. On the basis of Norman's dreams it was concluded that: 1) Norman had repressed most of the feelings he has toward his father; 2) the father is dead and was absent much of the time from the family; 3) the father is bisexual and probably seduced his son; 4) Norman has always considered his father dangerously impulsive, and that the father was more hostile than nurturant toward his son; and 5) Norman's sister was the father's favorite. Norman's history and perceptions agree with these conclusions in every detail. They indicate the intensely negative impressions which Norman had of his father and agree with those findings of the dream analysis which suggest the central importance of that relationship for Norman's subsequent maladjustment.

These findings, whose certainty is established by a remarkable agreement between variously derived data, are not dissimilar to what other investigators have found in a more piece-meal fashion regarding child molesters. One of the two major studies conducted in this area was carried out in the Forensic Clinic of the Toronto Psychiatric Hospital (Mohr, Turner, and Jerry, 1964), and the other by the Institute for Sex Research of Indiana University (Gebhard, Gagnon, Pomeroy and Christenson, 1965). The Toronto investigators conclude that "the pedophilic act represents an arrested development in which the offender has never grown psychosexually beyond the immature prepubertal stage, or a regression or return to this stage due to certain stresses in adult life, or a modification of the sexual drive in old age" (p. 19).

The question of fixation (arrested development) versus regression on Norman's part has already been discussed. The tentative conclusion was reached that he never grew up psychologically. Of course this does not preclude the influence of stress in adult life from exacerbating his condition. The Toronto investigators also note the pedophile's relative isolation from adult social contacts and the immature level of his sexual gratifications. He looks and exhibits, fondles and is fondled but rarely consummates the sexual act.

Of particular interest were the attempts of the investigators at the Institute for Sex Research to classify "heterosexual offenders against children" more precisely (defined operationally as adult males who had been convicted for sexual contact with female children, not their daughters, which did not involve the use of force or threat of force). Certain of these classifications are useful in an attempt to describe and to understand Norman. Those classified as "pedophiles" were often found to have reasonably adequate sexual relationships with women at the same time that they were engaging in sexual contacts with children (and in which affection was usually not involved). These persons were not characterized by feelings of inferiority or insecurity or shyness. Clearly Norman would not fit into this classification. Others were classified as "mental defectives," and Norman could not be so described. Still others were termed "amoral delinquents" whose behaviors appeared to be a function of a lack of conscience. These persons tended to act out their sexual impulses without reference to the sexual object, although their sexual contact with a child was apt to be a one-time impulsive act. Ordinarily there was no sexual deprivation in terms of their past sexual contacts with women, and only most infrequently was there ever any evidence of inferiority feelings or guilt with respect to any of the sexual behaviors. This picture does not coincide with Norman's personality or the history of his sexual experiences. Others were classified as "psychotics" who acted out sexually with children only during their psychotic episodes. These persons were found to have adequate sociosexual relationships with adults during those times that they were not psychotic. Norman's history does not coincide with this description either. Norman *does,* however, appear much like the kind of person whom the Indiana investigators have termed "sociosexually underdeveloped." Such persons never had heterosexual experience which would have been appropriate for their age. They suffered from feelings of extreme inferiority and shyness with persons of the opposite sex. Their sexual contacts with children (in the case of Norman, his compulsive voyeurism) were considered simply a continuation of childhood sex play and preoccupations. There is no question but that these investigators would have assigned Norman to this particular group, again, confirming the strongest impressions which our data give of Norman—that his sexuality reflects *chiefly* an infantile fixation and not a psychosis or a sociopathic personality, even though there may be elements of both which enter in.

Smaller scale studies of child molesters have also revealed their infantile character structure. Kielholz (1951) found infantile behavior and delayed physical and emotional development in one case he studied. Stricker (1967) had 64 male pedophiles rate the Blacky pictures on 21 scales of the semantic differential. Their responses indicated an immature and feminine orientation. A study of 120 male pedophiles in San Quentin (Torbert, Bartelme, and Jones, 1959) ascertained that they had rather strong religious interests and were inadequate in interpersonal relations. Finally, Cutter (1958) has argued that recidivism in sexual psychopaths may be due, in part, to their inability to cope with life outside an institution. Their return to the institution is experienced as relief.

This picture of the pedophile as an infantile character is identical with the one which has been derived from Norman's dreams. Our study does, however, go beyond any of the previous studies in identifying and describing the specific variables that constitute the infantile character of one pedophile, and in attempting to discover the origin of his pregenital fixation.

From our data, Norman's molestations can be viewed in many different ways: 1) the reenactment of a relationship he sought with his sister; 2) an attempt to recapture a spontaneity which he might have experienced in an asexual, infantile state; 3) Norman's fixation at a stage of psychosexual development due to his mother's intimacy; 4) an opportunity for Norman to pursue sociosexual relationships that require no commitment or competition and aggressive strivings on his part; 5) Norman's attempt to answer the questions he has had about the meaning of gender, and particularly his own. Put in still other ways, Norman's sexual predilections can be understood as: 1) a negative fixation that resulted from his mother's extreme reaction to the curiosity he had about his sister's genitals; 2) the rejection of sexual relations with male or female adults which, because of the earlier relationships he had with both parents, were endowed with threatening, incestuous qualities; 3) a function of his own identity diffusion which made it difficult for him to determine whether he was male or female, child or adult; 4) a way for Norman to compensate for the loss of self-esteem which he experienced in his relations with adults; and 5) the occasion for behaviors on his part which he—regardless of how other people defined them—considered to be more tender than sexual. The variety of motivations which maintained Nor-

man's behaviors is revealed by the present study to an extent
and at a depth which can be found in no other investigation
which has been conducted in this area.

Areas of Disagreement

The principal areas of disagreement, or at least differences in
emphasis, between Norman's dreams and the other data,
have to do with the following topics: 1) preoccupation with
the body; 2) failure of control; and 3) externalized superego.
From the dreams Norman appears to be preoccupied with
the central zones of his body (excluding the brain) and,
among other things, it was suggested that he might have had
sexual relations with his sister and enjoyed his sexual contacts in prison. The other data tend to refute these suppositions. Norman denies having had sexual relations with his
sister, and his sexual experiences in an institution, according
to him, were infrequent and lacking in affect. The case material, on the whole, tends to present an opposite picture of
Norman's relationship with his body. Although Norman's
dreams indicate (agreeing with the other data) that he takes
pride in controlling his sexual thoughts or actions, that his
impulsivity does not extend to the oral sphere (no special
interest in food or alcohol), and that he is unable to hold a
job, other findings or suppositions based upon Norman's
dreams are not supported. Norman has not been a
bedwetter, either at home or in an institution. Norman is
not a chronic masturbator. In fact whenever he masturbates
he feels depressed for a period of one or two weeks: "I
always feel I've lost something precious, like a man would
feel if he dropped a diamond into the water." Norman does
not lead a disorderly life. At the present time at least Norman
postpones gratification to an unusual degree. It would appear
that when it comes to Norman's failure to control his impulses, the dreams reflect Norman's urethral and anal eroticism during childhood which led to his urinating and defecating at the wrong times and places and which resulted in a
severe rejection by his peers. The dreams catch, as the other
data do not, Norman's extreme preoccupation with elimina-

tive functions which were at one time associated with interpersonal difficulties. Finally, where one might conclude from Norman's dreams that he tends to be psychopathic, that Norman relies, for example, on the Catholic Church as a kind of external superego, the other data present the picture of a schizoid personality whose flattened affect would account for shallow feelings of any kind including guilt, and of a person who has found it difficult to identify with any individual or group, including the Catholic Church whose claims he rejected long ago. These differences between what appears in Norman's dreams and in his waking life deserve further discussion.

If one were to juxtapose the contributions of the dream and other data to an understanding of Norman, one would have to say that whereas the body dominates the dream material, it is the mind and its gyrations which overshadow everything else in the other material.

Norman's preoccupation with his own and others' bodies, his tendency to view the world of men and machines in terms of what has been called a body ego, his chief engagement with the world on a basis established by the body's needs and activities: these aspects of Norman's perspective loom large in the content of his dreams. The primitive features of that perspective become even more pronounced in a display of issues and their solutions which are unusual for an adult. His activities, often those associated with an anal fixation, appear to be conducted with a wild abandon and in the most inappropriate contexts. Every aspect of his environment is endowed with an erotic potential, and much of the time he appears to be engaged with others on the basis of that potential. Urination, defecation, copulation, bodily stimulation with a host of "inappropriate" characters appear to be the chief components of Norman's behavioral repertoire. The id and its transactions are hardly disguised, seldom renounced. The presence and power of Norman's seething impulsivity in a world which reflects a similar lack of self-containment is attested to in his dreams as nowhere else. Reading Norman's dreams is like walking through a mire of filth and flesh.

The other data do not begin to cast the same kind of light

upon the bedrock of Norman's psychic structure. They are derived from sources once removed from his psychic origins, from processes that have evolved from an original, primitive experience and which they are designed to obscure. Norman's test responses as well as the account he gives of his behaviors and their motivations are the end points of a filtering process presided over by the ego and fortified by the superego. Masculine or feminine genital imagery is denied in the productions of his waking life. Anal events are hardly recalled; they have been replaced, for the most part, by concerns over order and the details of life. Without the dreams informing us, all that would be known about Norman would be the barely audible echo of that din which prevails intrapsychically.

This is not to say, however, that the muted sounds provided by these other data are not of crucial importance for our consideration of Norman's personality. Norman is more than id, and it is here that the outstanding difference between the dream and other data appears. An analysis of the dream content reveals very little about his defensive maneuvers. Reference is made to the shallowness of Norman's feelings, and it is surmised that he is functioning in accordance with an inadequate ego and an externalized superego. The weakness of his defenses is taken for granted, and the notion of his intellectualization or his capacities for sublimation comes in response to a specific question. The other data, however, as already noted, shed more light on Norman's control of his impulses than on any other aspect of his personhood. They point up his obsessive-compulsiveness, emphasize Norman's disengagement from his body, and his sublimation in intellectual curiosity, make much of the deep incongruence which exists between his thoughts and feelings, revealing, as the dreams do not, the pervasiveness of Norman's inhibitions and defenses.

There is, of course, some evidence in the dreams themselves of the kinds of control revealed in the other data. For example, there is Norman's refusal to take the passive role in an act of pederasty, the failure by another patient to have a sexual affair with him, Norman's feelings of euphoria associated with the knowledge that he has not had an orgasm, the presence of nuns which interrupts on two occasions the sexual advances he makes towards a young girl, his attempt to keep from becoming sexually aroused when he sees the panties of a five year old girl, and his concern about fires that will get out of control in the buildings topped by smokestacks. Norman's control is especially evident in those dreams which contain any heterosexual imagery:

> I was in a store. A saleslady asked me if I wanted to pay a woman to sleep with her. I said I was afraid of contracting venereal disease.

> A woman had a physical abnormality. We became intimate, but I did not feel sensation during the act.

> I was interrupted in something I was doing. Later, I was trespassing. Then, there was something about being in love.

Final Comments

The phallic imagery in Norman's dreams demonstrates a fundamental and recurring conflict: the need to overcome an insufferable sense of impotence and inferiority by an assertiveness which is equally threatening. Fears of castration by others or even by himself are followed by equal fears about the consequences of a potency which has not been defused:

> A man who owned a fish market was showing a movie at his store about how he traveled the country to get his fish. I showed him a transparent fish. He said he would return shortly to examine it. Before he returned, the fish shriveled up.

> I came to a motor powered paper cutter. Someone said it was for killing fish. The fish would trip a switch, releasing the blade which then came down upon the fish. It needed some glycerin. I went to get some.

> I was carrying a gun in my pocket. I tried to adjust it so it would not bulge from my pocket.

I was told that I would be released on parole. But the meat from a small bone on the table had to be scraped off first.

Whether or not sexuality and aggression are the most problematic features of civilized man's existence, they are certainly the chief issues in the life of our dreamer. In Norman they are hardly separate issues; the one is no more or less eschewed than the other. If one gives in to one *or* the other, one's lifesaving control is forfeited. "Death" comes as quickly and easily in orgasm as in anger.

Although the low incidence of weapons and the high proportion of non-aggressive encounters with others in Norman's dreams have been noted, explicit fears relating to aggression are also expressed in the dream material:

I was in a state of anxiety throughout the dream. I saw a man lying on the floor, shot.

I had a jack knife. It fell out of my hand onto the porch below. I heard someone gasp down there, and I was afraid the knife had hurt someone.

I was a patient in a hospital. I was going to be released. I accidentally hit a young patient in the face. I was excused. Later, I accidentally poked another patient in the face. He thought that I had done it purposely. I was afraid that I would not be released because of the incident. I asked to see the doctor so I could explain that it was an accident.

Norman seems to equate sexuality with aggression and both with a loss of control which endangers himself as well as others. There are aggressive as well as erotic elements to Norman's anal rebellion. By withholding his feces and defecating in inappropriate settings, Norman simultaneously thwarted his mother's will, secretly delighted in his anal eroticism, and deposited a contempt for his unrewarding immediate environs. And presumably others' punishing responses to his untimely acts reinforced the sado-masochistic features of Norman's interchange with the world. In most of his interpersonal transactions — whether they occur in his dreams or his waking life — Norman is the passive victim, and any occasion which suggests the assumption of a different role is avoided by an immobilization produced by equal measures of repulsion and attraction. The female genitals are a stimulus which elicits aggressive feelings in him ("The first time I saw female genitalia I felt like a tiger that had caught its prey.") and for that reason are avoided by a voyeurism which reflects his immobilized state or by a seduction for which he claims no responsibility or by the sexual activities of a pedophile which he can believe are more platonic than erotic. It must be remembered that he renounced his pedophilic activities only when they could no longer contain his equally renounced aggressiveness.

Of considerable interest is the correspondence of Norman's apparent lack of aggressiveness, his masochism, and his experience of castration, to what others might suppose is the female's experience of self and others. If the dreams and other data had not indicated otherwise, it might have been concluded that the chief issues in Norman's life pertained to his confusion over his gender identity. That this is not the case suggests that more attention must be given to the possibility that human behavior can be understood as more a function of fears concerning new experiences of the self and of others than concerns about gender or conflicts between the self and the ideal self. While Freud and other theorists offer constructs which pertain to the human disinclination to "grow up," none really focuses upon the extent to which this is possible, upon the trauma of new inputs, upon the human insistence that an original experience of the world be maintained. Perhaps one of the chief contributions of the present study is that it suggests a human being's behavior can be explained in large part as the result of fixation at an exceedingly primitive level, in which other issues such as gender identity or the claims of conscience are quite beside the point.

Another important contribution is an understanding of the way in which dreams reveal what is being defended against in waking behavior. Waking life may consist largely of defensive behavior—as Roheim spoke of culture as a massive defensive operation. Dreams tell us what the tasks are that waking behavior tries to solve, usually through displacements, symbolizations, reaction formations, projections, sublimations, negations, inhibitions, and repressions. It is only when defenses break down that the raw wish is revealed.

SIX

Norman's Present and Future

Norman was released from the veteran's hospital in late spring, 1966. He has not been hospitalized since. After he returned home, Norman made arrangements to pursue his education at a local community college where he has obtained an Associate in Arts degree. He is continuing his education at a local university where he hopes to receive a bachelor's degree which will enable him to go on to graduate study. Thus he remains a "perpetual student," spending much of his leisure time in the school library or in his own bedroom, studying at home doing the two things — reading and writing — which he really enjoys. It is interesting to note, and perhaps indicative of an improved psychological adjustment, that Norman is beginning to enjoy biographies. Most of his life he had not appreciated stories about people because people had seemed "unnatural" and "artificial."

At home Norman has little contact with either his mother, who spends most of her time tending the lawn or looking over the bills, or with his sister, who works on the assembly line of a local industry and spends her leisure time watching television. Although they take their meals together, do the shopping together, and go to church as a family, one gets the impression that in fact each has gone his separate way, bound together by a lethargy or a mutual dependency which makes any alternative arrangement unthinkable. They will probably continue to live together in this way until Norman's mother dies. After that, it is difficult to say what will happen or who will assume her role and function in her children's lives. Neither Norman nor his sister has been prepared for life without their mother, and it is difficult to predict what adjustments will be made when the time comes that she is no longer with them.

Of the two children, it is Norman who has made more of an attempt to enter into relationships with people outside the home. At school Norman has begun to make satisfying social contacts, particularly with older, married females. He has lunch with his fellow students in the school cafeteria and has come to enjoy discussing academic matters with them. Norman has received average grades in his courses, and there is every reason to believe that he will complete his course work satisfactorily.

With regard to his current psychological adjustment, Norman reports that he is rarely depressed or very unhappy, bored, or restless. However, he often feels very lonely or remote from other people. He has no psychosomatic complaints and rates his health at the present time as good. He does not appear to worry a great deal, but when he does it is usually about his future plans as well as his loneliness. There are other concerns as well. He writes, "I have experienced emotional distresses, periods of feelings of aimlessness and uselessness, stemming mainly from the difficulty I am having in distinguishing which of my experiences of the unusual type are in the long run going to be harmful to me and which are going to be beneficial. I feel great forces within my organism, and I do not want any of them to serve any immature desires that lead to self-destruction rather than the self-actualization that I seek." Another letter indicates that residues of his past torments remain: "I am attending _____ University now. I still have the same sexual 'hang-ups' that I had at _____ College. The mini skirts and the small panties under them still remind me that I am caught in the web of 'civilization.' I still have a longing to break from this web, the same longing that I had in those high school days when I used to read those dog stories like Jack London's *Call of the Wild*. I want to go where I can communicate telepathically with the animals, and know the freedom to be wild." Norman's recent correspondence reflects a continuing consternation over sexual interests which he can neither accept nor understand. Describing the central character in a novel which he had finished reading, he writes: "The hero is part brute as he peeps into a woman's room and watches her undress, and at times the hero is human as he sees two lovers and senses their pathos, their tenderness and their uncertainty; and he loathes the animal in himself. When he sees the swaying dresses of the women, it is not sexual intercourse that he wants, but 'some indefinable freedom of which the women, with their veiled and hidden nakedness, are a symbol.' This hero is so much like myself that when I read it, a surge of emotion came upon me." He refers, in another letter, to an article he had read on male voyeurism: "Sexuality exhibits the characteristic of tension caused by inadequate information and causes curiosity and conflict. The female with her internal genitalia poses an enigma for the male. Her upright posture and pubic hair prevent him from seeing her genitalia—further stimulating his curiosity." Clearly, Norman's present life includes issues and questions which have not been resolved either intellectually or emotionally.

Norman keeps up with politics in magazines, newspapers, and television. Although he sometimes votes in local elections, he is not politically active. On most issues of the day he would call himself a liberal. He is an independent voter, belonging to neither party. Norman goes to church with his mother and sister every week, even though he gives Zoroastrianism and Hinduism as his present religious preference. This illustrates his disinclination to refuse the requests his mother makes of him even now that he has reached middle age. His independence remains unexpressed. One of their most serious and open confrontations involved his determination to attend school fulltime. Although she considered this a waste of time and strenuously objected to these educational pursuits, Norman remained adamant.

More recently a disagreement arose between Norman and his mother with regard to the publication of the present book. Norman had known from the very beginning that such a book would be written and to this end had given his complete cooperation, meeting with Bell from time to time whenever additional information was needed. Often Norman would take the initiative himself, writing to Bell whenever he felt that certain matters pertaining to his past needed further clarification. It was in the spirit of what had become, over the years, a collaborative undertaking that Bell invited Norman to review the manuscript. However, Norman's mother, in characteristic fashion, opened the letter addressed to her son, read its contents, and then insisted that Norman join with her in an effort to have absolute control over every aspect of the report. Despite his own feelings on the matter, Norman enclosed a letter with his mother's list of demands which indicated that he agreed with his mother's statements. At the same time, in other private communications with Bell, Norman wrote: "My mother is upset about the book. She thinks that you are taking advantage of me. And she wants to read the book, because if anything is in it about her, she wants to have it omitted if she would rather not have it published or if, in her opinion, it is false. She says that I have no head for business, and always let people swindle me. She says it's been like that ever since I let my father bully me into not telling her what he did that day when I was four years old. . . No use trying to convince mother that I am competent enough to handle my affairs. All letters sent to me must be read by mother. I wrote that letter to appease mother, not because I agree with her." In subsequent letters Norman made it clear that he supported the publication of the manuscript. They also provide evidence of Norman's increasing dissatisfaction with his present home situation and of Norman's increasing attempts to establish viable relationships with others outside the home. For example, he writes to Bell: "Dear Alan: I hope you don't mind my addressing you by your first name. Since the encounter with my mother (over the publication of the manuscript), I feel more close to you." In a more recent letter, he makes the following disclosures: "Here is something that may surprise you: Last February, I wrote to a woman in reply to an ad in the personal column of a newspaper. Her ad said she was lonely, and wanted an acquaintance with a man interested in astrology or E.S.P. She is nine years older than I am. . . I received her reply about a week after the Easter mail strike. . . I replied to two of her letters and received a third one. I sent her a polaroid snapshot and she has sent me one of her. She has confided with me that she is in a state of sadness, confusion, and indecision. She had written something about this in an earlier letter. This is one reason for my pensive mood. I am afraid that as we correspond further, she may be disappointed in me or I may find things about her which are disappointing. I would welcome your advice regarding this relationship. . . Another thing depresses me. There is a meeting on E.S.P. that I would like to attend. If only I lived alone, I would certainly go there, since my final exams have been cancelled due to the strike. But my mother would never hear of it."

Norman is probably more independent of his mother than at any other time in his life. How much more independent Norman will become remains to be seen. Needless to say, it will not be an easy accomplishment.

When a record of dreams is kept by a person over a period of years, it is customarily found that what he dreams about does not change substantially in any systematic way from year to year. The usual consistency in a person's dreams over time has also been found in Norman's dream production.

There are, however, a few systematic changes which do occur over the three and one-half years that Norman recorded his dreams and which deserve attention.

With regard to characters, the proportion of females in Norman's dreams decreases, and the proportion of males increases over the five year period. Norman is becoming more like other males in having a higher proportion of male characters than female characters in his dreams. Part of the decrease in the number of females is due to the decreasing appearances of his mother. Both of these changes might be thought of as constituting an improvement in Norman's condition to the extent that they reflect a greater adult male identification and a diminution of Norman's dependency needs.

On the other hand, the proportion of familiar characters steadily decreases and the proportion of unfamiliar characters steadily increases over the five year period. A large number of strangers appearing in dreams is usually interpreted as representing a dreamer's alienation or isolation from people. If this interpretation is valid, then Norman's dream record indicates that he may be jumping from the "frying pan" of dependency into the "fire" of alienation. Alienation may increase the strain upon his infantile character to such an extent that even worse problems are precipitated. Unless his ego and superego are strengthened, he may find that living in a world of strangers, unprotected by family and friends, is intolerable. There is a systematic increase in the proportion of dreams in which Norman suffers a misfortune. If this indicates increasing self-punishment by an internalized superego, it could be a good sign, and one could consider this a transition phase from which Norman will emerge with a stronger and more effective personality. There is, however, no strong indication of this in his dreams at the present time. And the fact that the proportion of minors in Norman's dreams does not change over the five year period provides no grounds for optimism. In addition, sexual encounters with males and with minors actually *increase* while those with females *decrease*. Although there are those who would scarcely interpret this as progress, it may be that a homosexual orientation is evolving which represents a kind of maturity that is lacking in his pedophilic history.

Although the references in Norman's dreams to his mother decreases, the number of aggressive interactions with her increases, and the number of friendly interactions with her decreases. Friendly interactions with his sister also decrease. This could be interpreted as a good sign if it were balanced by fewer aggressions and more friendliness with other characters. But it is not. To lose affectional and dependency ties with the nuclear family can only be beneficial if positive cathexes are established with other adults. There is no indication in Norman's dreams of this taking place.

There is only one systematic change in the objects categories. The proportion of references to communication objects steadily rises from 1963 to 1967. This could represent an increasing need to communicate with others or else a diversion (sublimation) of libido into reading and writing activities. This is evident in his present style of correspondence and in his determination to pursue his higher education. If such a sublimation could be effected, it would probably offer the best chance Norman has for bringing about a real improvement in his condition. There is evidence from his most recent correspondence that Norman is attempting to move in this direction. He writes, "I am considering preparing some article or book that perhaps I could get published. I don't expect to complete anything of more than about ten pages, but it would be a start... Next Fall, I'm determined to join the Sensitivity Group at _____ University. This semester I kept putting it off until when I did get enough courage to act about it, it was after Easter and too late to join. The emotional intimacy kind of frightens me away, but I'm sure it would be rewarding." Norman will probably remain an infantile character, but this does not necessarily present a handicap for a writer, particularly if he addresses himself to themes which express his wishes and concerns. Were Norman younger it might be possible for a therapist to transform him into a reasonably well socialized, independent, heterosexual adult. This does not appear to be a present possibility for Norman.

With regard to Norman's sexual proclivities, the Toronto investigators found that the peak of pedophilic activity occurs from the mid to late thirties. Norman is now past this age, and this should be an opportune time for him to divert his interests into substitute channels while his impulses are in a relatively quiescent state. The same investigators found another peak of pedophilic activities in late adulthood and at the onset of old age. Such behaviors, however, are conducted by males with predominately heterosexual histories and who are motivated by concerns to which Norman is well-nigh a stranger. But even if there were an onslaught of impulses which occurs when Norman reaches that age, it is possible that defenses developed between now and then will effectively contain them.

Finally, another reason to believe that the future will not present new crises for Norman is the fact that he is not predominantly an oral character. He is not prone to use alcohol in order to allay his anxiety or to bolster a diminished masculinity. If Norman were an oral and not predominately an anal character, there would be little reason to hope for more than the chaos and confusion which he has known in the past. But because the anal mode is productive and potentially creative, at the present time there is reason to believe that Norman may be able to manage his future circumstances more adequately than he did in the past.

A Special Postscript

In the Spring of 1970, Norman wrote a letter to Bell which included his own appraisal of his past and present circumstances. Because they indicate a spirit which is quite remarkable, given the difficulties Norman has known and the effort which his current psychosocial adjustment requires, portions of that letter serve as "a special postscript" to the material that has preceded it.

I often wonder how I would have lived my life if my father had not sexually assaulted me that day when I was four years old. I probably would have gotten a doctorate in my 20's, then married and had a family. I would have bought a home and a car, and "lived happily ever after." I would have been a loyal Roman Catholic, never questioning the "truths" of the Church, never trying to experience for myself the things the Church philosophizes upon but discourages the individual from seeking to find out for himself. . . You know the Bible story of how Jacob wrestled with the angel. His brother Esau would never wrestle with the unknown. He was the kind of man I probably would have been if my father had not molested me. My father forced me to be a Jacob and wrestle with the unknown mysteries of life and death. . . We must sometimes have the courage to face the unknown. . . Sometimes I'm glad my father did that to me. I'm happy being a Jacob and not an Esau.

Epilogue

Until the summer of 1970 there was little about Norman's mood or behavior that differed from what the foregoing chapters of this book describe. Norman had achieved an uneasy equilibrium by mounting massive defenses against impulses that were hardly apparent except in his dreams. He had remained at home where he attempted to withdraw from his mother's and sister's claims upon him, but at the same time, he had made very little effort to make meaningful human contacts with those outside the home. He continued to go to school and to seek refuge in intellectual pursuits that served as a substitute for and a denial of a feeling state that was too threatening for him to experience directly. He was out of touch with his feelings and apathetic in his relations with others. And so, despite the fact that Norman's dreams had indicated very little change in the nature of his libidinal investments or in his perceptions of himself or others, it was reasonable for us to suppose that, because of his age and general character structure, Norman might be able to maintain himself outside an institution, not become involved again in child molestations, and attain a level of adjustment that would not have been predicted from his tortured history. However, in July, 1970 Bell received a letter from Norman that indicated that his situation was more fluid than we had supposed:

> I do not regret that I confided in you about the woman with whom I have been corresponding. There is something else that I've decided to confide in you about. I have hesitated, because I've hoped it would work itself to a solution. There was a patient in ————, a black man, who was on my ward for about a year. He was very quiet and stayed by himself. He seldom spoke to me. . . . He has been out now several years, and I've sent a few letters. He sent me $25 when I told him about getting the associate in arts degree.

I suspected that he had sexual interests in me while we were in _____. The letter he wrote last month seems to verify it. He writes me to come to his apartment and tells of his amorous feelings toward me. The letter is scented with perfume. I'm puzzled as to whether he has a masculine or a feminine desire for me — or both.

I'm writing this because it has caused me a conflict in my friendship with Margarita [his female correspondent whose name has been changed in order to preserve her anonymity]. I don't know what is right for me.

There are so many other aspects of man's nature besides the sexual aspect, his aesthetic, moral, spiritual, social, political, and his intellectual nature. I must understand all of these if I am to succeed in my task of helping to make the world right. I can't stay obsessed with the sexual as though it were the only important thing.

P.S. . . . Sometimes such grotesque thoughts enter my subconscious. I saw the movie, *I am Curious Yellow*. Unlike other movies showing sexual intercourse, the man injects his organ into the woman's vagina while her back is to him. I read years ago that this is the best position for giving pleasure to the woman because her clitoris comes into better contact with the man's organ. When I see women at jewelry counters and I'm behind one I get aroused. A few nights ago, I dreamed that I saw a teddy bear on a store counter and put my organ between its legs from the rear, and I looked around to see if it was clear. A woman was nearby and I avoided her. Another recent incident was going up an escalator in a local railway station. I felt my organ pressed against the buttox of an attractive girl in front of me, and I was aroused. There is a large store near the college where women often crowd around the jewelry counters, and I've had temptations this Spring semester to go and get some pleasure from their bodies. The ultimate happening that made me decide to write you was Wednesday morning when I helped a boy about three or four years of age reach a sink in the men's room and I had an orgasm as I pressed against his buttox.

I'm trying to rise above all this sexual confusion and be able to know the aesthetic quality of Eros and not its grotesque side. Then I can go on toward doing something creative to make the world more right.

Apparently the issues that Norman had sought to avoid

were not to be denied: His homosexual interests, his sexual preoccupations, his anal eroticism, and finally, his pedophilic predilections. Although he still maintained that he wanted to "rise above all this sexual confusion," he appeared to be less inclined than before to avoid those occasions in which the full strength of his confusion and conflict would be experienced. Feelings whose intensity had been apparent only in his dreams appeared to be surfacing, and it was all that he could do to cope with them. In the next letter, written to Bell on October 1, he stated:

From September 17th until Monday, the 28th, I was in an ever-increasing state of emotional shock and turmoil, and I *very* nearly took my life. Only a superhuman effort is responsible for my still being alive. I am still in a state of anxiety about the future, but now at least I'm not so confused. I'll explain now what happened.

Margarita and I were getting very close. We often wrote of how we have the same kind of ideals and fears, and the same kind of lonely and sad past, and how now we see a brightness in the future for us.

On September 8th, I received her letter of September 5th. She replied to things I'd written and mentioned some interesting things about astrology and her horoscope. I sent two letters that week. We had been writing about twice a week. The next week there was no word from her. I thought at first maybe she moved like she said she might and was busy at a new job. I wrote three letters that week. When Friday came and no letter, I started to *panic!* What could have happened? Was she injured? Was she ill? Maybe she read my letters of the past week and decided I had too many conflicts to be able to give her my love. A few weeks ago she had a dream of a man who was a patient in a hospital room. She visited him. He had seven feet on one leg. She pitied him. Then a nurse came in and their eyes met and he seemed to be in love with her. Margarita left the room. She heard them talking from outside in the hall but couldn't make out what was said. I interpreted her dream. I told her that maybe the man was me and the nurse was my mother.

When she stopped writing, I was thinking of all those things. I was thinking maybe she has decided that I have a parental romantic tie and have a homosexual conflict (since I mentioned that colored man sending me the love letter). She herself has an emotional block that she can't quite pin down, she told me. It is something related to her mother. Her mother keeps appealing to her to stay with her, though they never communicate. Her mother has never shown her any real love or understanding. Her *father* understood her. He was a Scorpio like *me*. . . . She is looking for a man who can (and will) give her the love a woman deserves. And in her last letters she told me that I make her happy beyond her wildest dreams. I was so sure she saw me as the man who could give her the love she desired. It was a shock beyond my wildest imagination when she stopped writing, and the possibility that she'd left me loomed before me. Can you *imagine* what I went through? Driving away from home one day after not hearing from her, I was going about 35 miles an hour. A car suddenly appeared about 300 feet ahead. But instead of my foot going to the brake it went all the way down on the *accelerator!* I caught myself in time to keep from smashing into the back of the car. But wild thoughts kept coming. Why didn't I go ahead? How wonderful to feel my car in an intimacy of intercourse with the car ahead. Just like I would with Margarita as I held her in an embrace, joining our bodies. Then, one big crash, like an orgasm, and this life of uncertainty and frustration and confusion and loneliness would be *done with!*

And those energizers I have. . . I have jars of them. What a chance to end it all! Should I go into some wood and leave my identification at home so no one would know who died? But then *my family* would go through what *I'm* going through with Margarita. Alan, I never could go through that again, I'm sure.

The days went by and I kept going over in my mind what each of us wrote in our letters, trying to find why it had happened. Monday, the 21st I sent a certified letter to Margarita pleading for her to write if she can, saying, "I love you." Afterwards I took a triple dose of tafranil along with a big dose of an aphrodisiac I bought at the health store. . . . The days went by; students asked why I was in a daze. But something was *calming* me the later part of the week. Wednesday night I felt Margarita kiss my cheek. . . . But the reality that I had no letter yet still gripped me. And Saturday I sent another desperate letter. Friday, I had confided with a student, a close friend, and she helped me in my despair. If not for her, I may not have been alive to send that letter Saturday. On Monday, however, there were *two* letters from Margarita! She'd just received my letters. She began her letter with these words: "I cried when I got those letters. I had been through so much hell. I had about decided not to write you again." It turned out that my letters had nothing to do with her not writing. . . . What a change came over me. I was *alive* again. But things are not at all calm yet. Oh, Alan, I'm so frustrated, I want to help Margarita so bad, but I'm so helpless! What am I going to do? What if she doesn't write anymore now? Should I go to her home town and look for her? She's never sent me her home address, but I have a picture of her in front of her house near a trailer camp, and she lives in a small town. I was going to go there this weekend if I hadn't heard from her. I'd tell my mother that the science class was going to an exhibition upstate and staying over Saturday night.

Another thing on my mind is that she is not educated in literature, though she *is* interested in *everything*. That's what makes her seem so young. I had planned to marry a woman who could help me write creatively. As the cliche goes, "It's a great life if you don't weaken."

Again, some of the perspectives offered in the preceding sections of this book are forcefully revealed, not muted at all by repressive maneuvers used in the past. Norman's special but detested relationship with his mother, which has made viable cathexes with others outside the family all but impossible, is clearly evident. His association of violence with sex, which had led to his eschewal of both except in very ambiguous forms, is also quite apparent. His dependency (in this instance, on a kind of mother surrogate) and vulnerability are reflected in his relationship with Margarita. But of special interest, because it represents a departure from his former styles of psychological and social management, is Norman's attempt to reach out in unaccustomed ways for experiences that he would have avoided in the past. For the first time in his life he is strongly involved emotionally with a woman who is neither his mother nor his sister. He has made an investment in her that could not be found in his past relationships. And on the strength of that relationship he has begun to entertain the possibility of breaking away from his mother. In addition, we find Norman *seeking* opportunities for sexual experiences that, formerly, he would have avoided at all costs. His purchase of an "aphrodisiac" is perhaps the most dramatic evidence of those changes in Norman that are provided by our most recent correspondence. Norman's most recent letter, in answer to a letter sent by Bell in which he suggested that Norman get in touch with one of Bell's psychologist colleagues living not far from Norman and his family, indicates the strength of Norman's feelings, the changes that have occurred in his behaviors, and the nature of his present goals:

... Thinking over your letter of October 11th, I have been feeling melancholy. Surely, after all those dreams I showed you and the things about my deepest emotions that I've confided in you, you must have *some* understanding of the tragic nature of my present situation. I *know* you have *some* rapport with me. But your words distress me. You say that "letters to and from you and Margarita will probably not help very much at a time like this."

Perhaps I did not explain enough to impress you with the depth of my relationship with Margarita. I believe that letters to and from Margarita are the *only* things that can help me now. Don't you understand, Alan? *Margarita is like me.* She wants what I want. We have a deep passion for the forbidden. We must gratify that passion of ours or our lives will be without purpose. Of all the millions of people in the world, I've found someone I can be *close* to, someone who will experiment with me in sexual adventures and in mystical adventures, as we work out our lives together. All those years, Alan! All those years of yearning for the mystery under the female panty, the mystery of death—all those years of frustration! Now at last I've *found* someone who will help me penetrate into those mysteries of life. All those years, since 1962, probing into philosophy, theology, psychology, sociology, mysticism, and science trying to find an intellectual way to penetrate that forbidden heaven! My desire to find in *literature* an answer! *Experience* is what I need, Alan, not all that intellectual probing. That's what my body has been crying out for all these years. That's why I always want to have sexual adventures with children. Now I *have* someone, and I don't have to worry about the law condemning me. Can't you see why I just *can't bear* to lose her? I still feel attracted to children. I still look up the skirts. But now I see *Margarita* everywhere. It's *her* body I see. I've *found* someone. I've written her begging her to meet me somewhere within the next three weeks. . . . If only I could see her. I'd tell her about my past.

For the past month, I have been taking an aphrodisiac which I discovered at the Health and Diet Food Store last month. . . . As the days go by, this aphrodisiac is really beginning to affect me. I feel so lusty, so virile! When I had that orgasm with that boy, it was about three times as much as usual. And I didn't get the usual physical after-effects nearly as much, like the way my skin usually feels dry and my hair loses its lustre. Even the emotional after-effects were not strong in spite of my distress at being caught by the mother.

My body feels so warm and soft. And everyone else's feels so warm to me. I feel a great energy awakening inside me. I'm not so frightened about what may lie ahead, what sorrows, or whatever. . . . I believe I'm regaining some equilibrium on this tightrope called earthly life. I do need equilibrium but it must be a *dynamic* kind of equilibrium, not the static kind I would find in a hospital. Margarita, I'm certain, would be a fulfillment for me. . . . Pray for us.

P.S.: I read somewhere that if an aphrodisiac is taken before going to bed, the person has romantic dreams. I've tried it since then, and it has proven right. And another thing, now I awaken nearly every morning with a wonderful erection that lasts a long time before I have to urinate. I need a lot of self-will to keep from having orgasms during that time, and I have had them several times. When I was in the Army in Italy, I recall a man in my barracks who used to shout to the others sometimes after the reveille was sounded: "Boy! I woke up with a piss hard-on that chould choke a horse!" I know now what he means. I think of Margarita during those times. I just received a sweet letter from her. I'm so happy. She says she'll see me soon.

Norman appears to sense the price he has paid in the past for whatever psychological adjustment he was able to accomplish. He is not content with the ways in which he has managed not to fall from what he describes as the "tight-rope" of human existence. He now speaks of a "dynamic equilibrium" and is attempting to acknowledge and to integrate a range of feelings instead of rejecting them. In a recent visit Bell had with Norman it was apparent that Norman had not been altogether unsuccessful. He appeared to be more aggressive, more sociable, and more spontaneous than Bell had ever known him in the past. At the same time, it is reasonable to suppose that the less Norman is inclined to disavow his feelings, the greater becomes the possibility that he will act them out in ways that could have most unfortunate personal and social consequences. There is probably more reason to believe that this will happen than that a higher level of psychological and social adjustment will be reached by what he dares to experience at the present time. His relationship with Margarita is based more on fantasy than fact. And if he experiences rejection by her before the range of his other social contacts is greatly enlarged it is quite likely that he will once again turn to a child, even as his father turned to him. Norman's present situation is most precarious, and given all that has happened in the past and that accounts for a psychological status that had once been more apparent in his dreams than in his waking life, it is difficult to know the "worst" that can be anticipated.

SEVEN

The Value of Dream Analysis

Dreams have not been interpreted for their own sake in this present study. Our interest has not been in the psychology of dreaming, in how dreams are formed, or in the function of dreams. Rather, our aim has been to understand a person by means of analyzing a series of his dreams, using an objective and quantitative method of content analysis. The method yields frequency of occurrence (incidence) for each of a number of elements or categories (classes of elements). The essential operation performed in arriving at these incidences is that of counting.

The basic assumption of such an analysis is that incidence is a direct measure of the importance of that element in the life of the dreamer. If he dreams frequently of his mother, as Norman did, it is inferred that the mother plays an important role in his life. This may be called the *continuity* hypothesis because it assumes there is continuity between dreams and waking life. There are difficulties with this hypothesis as we have seen but first let us reconsider some of the kinds of information that dreams provide.

Dreams provide a lot of purely factual information about a person: his vocation, the members of his family, marital status, habits, interests, preferences, and hobbies. They also yield information concerning his personality traits, conflicts, complexes, and concerns. Since some of this information can be easily obtained by asking a person, it would appear to be unnecessary to go to the bother of analyzing 1,368 dreams merely to find out that Norman is unmarried, lives with his mother and sister, has an aunt who is a nun, likes to read and swim, had been arrested and convicted of molesting children, and is a printer by trade. Personality traits like aggressiveness, curiosity, and sociability can also be fairly easily determined by observing how a person behaves in waking life. Nor does one usually have to probe very deeply in order to get at his anxieties, conflicts, frustrations, and complexes. Thanks to Freud and Jung and their coworkers, the terrain of personality has been pretty well mapped so that we know what questions to ask and what to look for.

Of what value then is dream analysis? May it not be superfluous or outmoded? We believe not and for the following reasons. Consider, first, the purely factual information. Norman is a printer; dreams and waking life agree on this. What the dreams tell us, however, when they are subjected to content analysis is what this vocation means to him, its *phenomenology* if you please. Norman projects many of his concerns onto the printing press. A man's vocation is not merely a way of earning a living or spending his time. It is a stage on which he mounts his inner dramas. The external environment is animated with whatever animates one's inner life so that it might be said that subject and object in a psychological sense are one and the same.

Again, for example, Norman's dreams tell us that Norman is unmarried. But they also suggest *why* he is unmarried. It is this *why* of behavior—which in waking life is so often hidden by defenses, rationalizations, self-deceptions, and just plain ignorance—that dreams are so good at revealing. *Dreams are often visualizations of psychic phenomena that can only be imperfectly described verbally in waking life.*

The same rationale applies to personality traits and to complexes and conflicts. Not only can they be identified and explained by a content analysis of dreams, but their strength can be assessed. Everyone is to some extent a child in his dreams just as he is everything else that is set forth in a psychoanalytic textbook. This is called *the principle of universal man.* What makes a person an individual is the weight of each of these variables in his makeup. Freud stated the general hypothesis that is followed here in this manner: " . . . we are tempted to say that the elements of the psychic constitution are always the same. What changes in the mixture is the quantitative proportion of the elements and, we must add, their location in different fields of the psychic life and their attachment to different objects." (Freud, 1967).

Dreams also yield suggestive information about the probable origins of behavior. Dreams appear to tap the network of memories to an extent that no other readily available form of behavior does. They seem to have access to the remotest memories, even going so far apparently as to restore memories laid down during the fetal period (Hall, 1967). They do this without benefit of free association or amplification.

There are, however, some special considerations that should be kept in mind in using the method of content analysis on a series of dreams. The first such consideration is the *omitted element,* that is, an element with zero frequency. This is exemplified in the present study by the absence of the father from Norman's dreams. If the incidence of an element is considered a direct index of the significance of that element for the dreamer, then one would have had to conclude that the father had played an insignificant role in Norman's life. Just the opposite proved to be true. The father's behavior was decisive in Norman's development. In this instance, then, our basic assumption was invalidated, and needs to be qualified as follows. When a character whom one *expects* to find in a series of dreams—mother, father, wife, or children—has a zero frequency one should consider the possibility that the character has been repressed from the dreams. From our experience this qualification rarely has to be observed and probably only applies to members of the dreamer's immediate family and to basic impulses. For example, if Norman never had a sex dream one would immediately suspect that repression and not lack of interest was the explanation.

When there is reason to believe that repression has occurred then one should search for the representation of the repressed element in a symbolic or displaced form. For the father, these would be father figures — older males in positions of authority, and animals. In Norman's case, several dreams in which fathers (but not Norman's father) appeared and several in which animals were the central figures gave clues as to Norman's perceptions of his father.

Symbolism is pervasive in dreams although there seems to be wide differences in the extent to which various dreamers use symbols to represent their thoughts and feelings. We make it a rule in analyzing dreams to draw whatever inferences we can from direct expressions before considering displaced or symbolic representations. A few examples from Norman's dreams illustrate this. Norman's feelings and conceptions regarding his mother and sister were directly expressed in his dreams so that a straightforward content analysis was all that was necessary to establish their meaning for him. The same thing was true of Norman's sex dreams. This does not mean that sex was not also expressed in symbolic ways in one of Norman's dreams, but that their direct expression provided enough data to warrant the conclusion that Norman has a polymorphously perverse disposition. Norman's weak control over the eliminative functions were often depicted in his dreams, only thinly disguised as leaky pipes, fountains, floods, overflowing sinks, sewers, and mud. But there was also a lot of actual urinating and defecating.

This is the place to point out that symbolism is probably no less prevalent in waking life than it is in dreams. Each of us lives in a world that is charged with potent symbols of our inner life and bodily processes. We are so used to thinking in terms of purely utilitarian models of the objects and systems — political, economic, et cetera — that man has created and with which he interacts that we often fail to see their psychic significance.

Another consideration that needs sharper definition is the *use of norms* in content analysis studies. The frequencies obtained from an analysis of Norman's dreams were compared with frequencies obtained from a group of dreams reported by young men and a group reported by young women. From one point of view norms are not necessary. One can formulate a perfectly valid picture of a person without regard to the ways in which he is similar to or different from others. Often, however, the psychologist is dealing with a person who has a specific problem which differentiates him from most of mankind. He is a child molester, an alcoholic, or a schizophrenic. Then the question that the psychologist tries to answer is what there is about his personality and its development that may be responsible for or correlated with his specific condition. What differentiates a child molester from those who are not? In order to answer this question norms are necessary. That Norman was unduly preoccupied with interior space in his dreams could only be determined by comparing the incidence of buildings, rooms, etc. in his dreams with norms. It was decided that orality was not a significant feature of Norman's aberrant behavior, because the incidence of oral incorporative dreams was no greater than that of the norm group. It was also possible to show that Norman had some feminine identification because some of his frequencies were more like the norms for women than the norms for men.

How many dreams are required in order to make a content analysis? One can obtain important information about a person from a content analysis of as few as twenty-five dreams. The analysis of Freud's and Jung's personalities were based on 28 dreams and 31 dreams, respectively. A great deal was learned about Kafka from 37 of his dreams. Undoubtedly, it was not necessary to have 1,368 of Norman's dreams in order to arrive at a formulation of his personality. One advantage of having a large number of dreams is that the incidence of even infrequently mentioned elements is large enough to provide useful information. For example, one expects to find three overt sex dreams in a series of twenty-five dreams reported by a young adult male, or twelve in a series of one hundred dreams. Twelve or even three such dreams tell us something about the nature of the dreamer's sexual attitudes and preferences. If some of the twelve dreams, for example, involved a homosexual relationship it would signify that the dreamer had homosexual inclinations. Or if in the bulk of the sex dreams, the dreamer was witnessing but not otherwise participating in the activity it would suggest he had voyeuristic tendencies. But it would take more than twelve dreams to establish with certainty the range of sexual interests and behaviors which was found in Norman's 1,368 dreams. One would expect on the basis of the norms to find 164 dreams out of the 1,368 which could be scored for sexual content. Norman actually had 176 such dreams which is only a chance deviation from the expected number. By classifying these 176 sex dreams according to age and gender of the sexual partner an unassailable picture of Norman's many-sided sexual proclivities emerged.

There is one final consideration in drawing inferences about a person's waking behavior from his dreams which should be mentioned. It is important to distinguish between preoccupation and what is called acting out. The distinction may be clarified by the following example. If a person has a lot of dreams in which he is quarreling or fighting with other characters one would conclude that he is an aggressive person in waking life. Usually this is the case. Aggression in dreams tends to mirror aggression in waking life. Sometimes, however, aggressiveness in waking life does not manifest itself in overt behavior but expresses itself in private fantasy and thought. Failure to act out aggression is explained in terms of ego defenses and superego restraints. It might even happen that there was a strong reaction formation so that in waking life a person would appear over-friendly, deferential, and solicitous of others. In such cases, it might be concluded that dreams were compensating for what a person lacked in waking life.

Actually, however, this apparent lack of correlation or inverse correlation between how a person acts in his dreams and how he acts in waking life is rare. When it does occur, one can usually discover all kinds of subtle and not so subtle indications of how the dream behavior expresses itself in fantasy or displacements or reaction formations in waking life. As Freud observed, a person eventually gives himself away. To an observant eye, there are few secrets.

One might turn the question around and ask why a person who acts out his impulses during the day should dream about acting them out during the night. If dreams attempt to fulfill wishes that remain unfulfilled in waking life then why did Norman, a child molester, dream about molesting children? There are two parts to the answer. The first part is that a basic impulse is never completely satisfied, or if it is, the satisfaction is only temporary. Satiation gives way to hunger in a few hours. A millionaire wants to be a multimillionaire. Norman never "had" enough children. Instead of the thirty that he admitted to having "inspected" over a period of nearly twenty years three hundred or even three thousand "molestations" still would not have satisfied him. This brings us to the other part of the answer.

It can be stated as a general rule that any preoccupation is a preoccupation because the object or activity with which one is preoccupied is not and cannot be completely satisfying except for a very short time. This is because the object of desire—in Norman's case, children—is not the originally desired object. It is a displacement from some original object, and displacement can only be partially satisfying. Second best is never the best. Compulsions are usually fed from many sources. It is not that dreams fail to satisfy wishes; they fail to satisfy the original wishes. The same conslusion applies to waking behavior. That is why Norman could dream about molesting children as well as molest them in waking life or think about molesting them. The continuity hypothesis holds generally speaking because dreams and waking behavior are both motivated by the same unfulfilled impulses.

The accomplishments of this study are twofold. First, it has shown that an objective method of content analysis when applied to reported dreams yields important information about the personality and behavior of the dreamer. Second, it has identified some, if not all, of the components that go to make up the personality of a type of child molester. That is to say, it has taught us something about the *uses* of dreams and something about a particular class of offender.

References

1. Cutter, F. Recidivism in Sexual Psychopaths: Some Impressions. *Psychological Newsletter,* 1958, Vol. 10, pp. 28–32.
2. Freud, S. Three Essays on Sexuality (1905). In *The Standard Edition,* Vol. VII. London: Hogarth, 1953.
3. ———— Introduction. In Freud, S., and W. C. Bullitt. *Thomas Woodrow Wilson.* Boston: Houghton Mifflin, 1967.
4. Gebhard, P. H., J. H. Gagnon, W. B. Pomeroy, and Cornelia V. Christenson. *Sex Offenders: An Analysis of Types.* New York: Harper & Row, 1965.
5. Gerbner, G. et al., Ed. *The Analysis of Communication Content.* New York: Wiley, 1969.
6. Hall, C. S. Strangers in Dreams: An Empirical Confirmation of the Oedipus Complex. *Journal of Personality,* 1963, Vol. 31, pp. 336–345.
7. ———— Are Prenatal and Birth Experiences Represented in Dreams? *The Psychoanalytic Review,* 1967, Vol. 54, pp. 99–105.
8. ———— Content Analysis of Dreams: Categories, Units, and Norms. In Gerbner, G. et al., Eds. *The Analysis of Communication Content.* New York: Wiley, 1969a. pp. 147–158.
9. ———— Normative Dream-Content Studies. In Kramer, M., Ed. *Dream Psychology and the New Biology of Dreaming.* New York: Thomas, 1969b. pp. 175–184.
10. Hall, C. S. and G. W. Domhoff. The Dreams of Freud and Jung. *Psychology Today,* June, 1968, pp. 42–45; 64–65.
11. Hall, C. S. and R. E. Lind. *Dreams, Life, and Literature: A Study of Franz Kafka.* Chapel Hill, North Carolina: University of North Carolina Press, 1970.

12. Hall, C. S. and R. L. Van de Castle. *The Content Analysis of Dreams*. New York: Appleton-Century-Crofts, 1966.

13. Kielholz, A. Perversion und Sexuelle Erziehung. *Psychol. Berater gesundes prokt. Lebensgesalt*, 1951, Vol. 3, pp. 452-458.

14. Mohr, J. W., R. E. Turner and M. B. Jerry. *Pedophilia and Exhibitionism*. Toronto: University of Toronto Press, 1964.

15. Stone, P. J., D. C. Dunphy, M. S. Smith, and D. M. Ogilive. *The General Inquirer: A Computer Approach to Content Analysis*. Cambridge, Mass.: The M. I. T. Press, 1966.

16. Stricker, G. Stimulus Properties of the Blacky to a Sample of Pedophiles. *Journal of General Psychology*, 1967, Vol. 77, pp. 35-39.

17. Thass-Thienemann, T. *The Subconscious Language*. New York: Washington Square Press, 1967.

18. _____. *Symbolic Behavior*. New York: Washington Square Press, 1968.

19. Torbert, S., K. F. Bartelme and E. S. Jones. Some Factors Related to Pedophilia. *International Journal of Social Psychiatry*, 1959, Vol. 4, pp. 272-279.

20. Van de Castle, R. L. Problems in Applying Methodology of Content Analysis. In Kramer, M., Ed. *Dream Psychology and the New Biology of Dreaming*. New York: Thomas, 1969. pp. 185-195.

Tests

1. Adjective Check List. Harrison G. Gough, author.
2. Edwards Personal Preference Schedule. Allen L. Edwards; Psychological Corporation.
3. Index of Adjustment and Values. Robert E. Bills, author.
4. Minnesota Multiphasic Personality Inventory, Revised Edition. Starke R. Hathaway and J. Charnley McKinley; Psychological Corporation.
5. Rorschach Inkblot Test, Grune and Stratton.
6. Rotter Incomplete Sentences Blank. Julian B. Rotter; Psychological Corporation.
7. Study of Values: A Scale for Measuring the Dominant Interests in Personality, Third Edition. Gordon W. Allport, Philip E. Vernon, and Gardner Lindzey; Houghton Mifflin Co.
8. Thematic Apperception Test. Henry A. Murray; Harvard University Press.
9. Wechsler Adult Intelligence Scale. David Wechsler; Psychological Corporation.

Appendix I

Further samples of Norman's dreams are listed below in the same order of topics found in Chapter three.

Polymorphously Perverse Disposition: Sexual Encounters

A man wanted me to take the passive role in an act of pederasty. I refused.

A woman was seated on the chair with me on my left, and a little girl was seated with me on my right. We were very crowded. I felt their thighs against mine, and it was a pleasurable feeling.

I was lying on a bed clad in shorts. I felt the nude body of a man below me. His organ was pressed against me. I was excited, and I pulled down my shorts. But when I felt below me with my hands, I did not feel anyone there even though I still felt his body against my backside.

A patient tried to persuade me to have a sex affair with him. I told him that I am heterosexual.

A patient on the ward who is a homosexual wanted me to be his "husband."

I saw a young boy. I wanted him to sit on my lap.

I was seated in an auditorium. I changed seats with a patient on the ward. Without saying anything, he touched my chest, then hugged me from behind.

I was in bed next to a patient. He asked me to put my foot between his thighs.

A man approached me and said that he liked my body.

... As she (a woman of 30) spoke I had a sudden urge to put my hand up her dress. I did so, and she had no underwear on. She resented what I had done, and I felt badly about it, so I apologized to her.

Sexual Concerns and Feelings

I was talking with a man whom I at first mistook for a doctor, but later saw was a judge. I told him I was sorry about committing the offense.

I was walking on a street. I was in a state of euphoria. Clairvoyant visions appeared before me. Then a little girl came and asked me to lift her. I lifted her and she thanked me. Then I had an emission, although I had no erection. I was dejected because I had not tried harder to control myself. The visions would not come anymore.

I was with a woman about 25. We dressed in swimming attire. Then she and I went to look for a secluded place where we could have sexual intercourse ... The woman and I became separated. Then I met my mother. She thought I was planning to steal something. I told her I was not, but I did not tell her about the woman I was looking for.

I was with a young woman and an older one. The young one seemed to be romantic. She made an affectionate gesture. The older woman was annoyed. A middle aged woman walked by and asked her if she was jealous.

I went down a road and came to a place where I had gotten into trouble for bothering a child. I tried to avoid being seen. I felt remorse for what I had done.

I met a dark haired woman about my age. We fell in love and kissed secretly in a downstairs room of her house. We had to keep out of sight of her mother. Her mother came in upon us, and she was angry about my advances. She said, "I know what kind of place you came from. Girls in bikinis." I replied that she had misjudged me.

A man who looked like the charge officer on my former ward came over to me and said he would help us. He said, "You know that it is a serious thing to molest a child, don't you?" I said, "Yes, I do."

I was looking up girls' dresses to see their thighs. A little girl was nearby, and I started to go to her, but a man was standing next to her, so I didn't go.

I was on a hospital porch with a nurse. I asked her something and she answered yes. As her lips parted, our lips were drawn together uncontrollably, and we kissed. After the kiss, she was upset because we had just met, but she was not angry at me. She was worried whether someone had seen us.

I was wandering through the streets. I saw a girl about 8, but I did not approach her, because I was afraid I would get into trouble.

Children were in the distance. I was tempted to approach them, but I resisted.

Fears of Sex and Aggression

I was driving a car, and a little girl stepped into the car's path. I hurt my knee trying to swerve to avoid her. I drove on, but a little later I stopped, and sat in the car reflecting on what a terrible thing had happened, and I was hoping that the girl was not hurt.

A girl about seven greeted me. . . I had a desire to hug her, but I thought how fragile she was, how a piece of iron from above her could crush her . . . .

Polymorphously Perverse Disposition: Voyeurism

A girl was there. I saw her panties.

I was in a dance hall. I saw the back of a young woman. I wondered how she looked in front, so I turned her around.

Two women came out clad only in panties. I wished they had been nude so I could see their organs.

I was lying on the floor looking through a mirror. I saw the reflection of two girls about 10 years old. I could see up their dresses and I enjoyed looking at their legs. They could not see me, but one of them turned my way and I feared that she was suspicious about something, or that I was exposed some way so that she saw me.

Three women about 25 were standing nude on sofas ... While they were unclad I studied the size and shape of the lips of their vulvas and tried to see how they reflected the girls' personalities.

Dependency

I was living in a house with my mother and sister. The house resembled one we lived in in _____. I lay on a high bed in a dimly lit room. The bed was by a window, and I looked out into the yard. I felt very nostalgic as I looked out, as I recalled living there before.

My mother, sister and I bought a house and went there to live.

My mother and I were looking at a garage with a high gable. Then she and my sister went to a resort with a lake surrounding it. I did not go because I had been there before. After they had left I wished I had gone with them.

I was with my mother in a Latin country. We were in a nightclub. My mother took some phonograph records upstairs to sell them. A man said it wasn't allowed. I was worried about getting into trouble but my mother came downstairs and said the woman upstairs said she would keep us from getting into trouble. We went outside. Shrubbery was around the building. I was nostalgic when we passed some place that reminded me of an emotional and spiritual experience in the past. We met my sister. A black cat appeared, and we were nervous because of the bad omen. The cat had a head like a dog. We petted its head.

I was putting together rectangular pieces of various colors. My mother and sister were helping me.

I was in a theatre with my mother and sister, watching a stage show. When it was over, my mother said we had better hurry because we had an appointment somewhere. We walked outside the theatre past a fountain. My mother kept telling my sister and I to hurry.

I was with my mother in a big house with an outsized fireplace. My mother was papering the walls. She needed something and I went to get it. She did not like something I did.

I lived in a strange house with my mother and sister. I went outside and lay by the basement window. My sister was in the basement. My mother saw me, and thought I was eavesdropping on my sister and she scolded me.

New rules were made in the hospital where I was a patient. My mother and sister could not visit me anymore.

I was visiting _____ with my mother and sister after being away for a long time.

. . . a boy . . . had been at our house annoying my mother. I told him he'd better stay away from the house. He laughed and said, "Did your mother tell you to say that?" I replied that my mother does not tell me to do things.

I was in a hospital. My mother visited me and talked about how serious murder is.

My mother warned me about something.

I kissed a little girl on the lips. In a later dream, I was scolded by my mother about something. She was very upset.

I was going somewhere with my mother. She became impatient about something. She said to me that I was better twenty years ago, and said, "Why can't you be like you were then?"

I was living in an unfamiliar house. My mother tied my ankles to the bed as I lay on my back, so that I would not get upset.

I was getting ready to take a boy on a trip to a quay. My mother was helping me.

I was in a house I lived in. I picked up a book, and some photos and papers with prayers printed on them fell out of it. As I was picking them up I heard my mother talking outside with my sister. I was relieved to hear their voices. A sudden fear came upon me that the next time my mother left, something would prevent her from returning.

I had built a wheel barrow to carry ice packed in bags. I did not know where to deliver the ice. Then, my mother came and gave me a coin to telephone about the ice.

Dependency: Sibling Relationship

I was in a room with my sister. We were in separate beds. She showed me the lower part of her body.

I was in a house with my mother and sister. I noticed a rip in my sister's bed sheet and tried to mend it with adhesive tape. My sister saw me and wondered what I was doing. She became excited and called mother.

My mother and I were looking for my sister. We found her in a ditch about 5 feet deep. She was depressed, and we cheered her up.

Someone had assaulted a little girl sexually and my sister thought I had done it. I told her I did not do it. At first she doubted me. Then she said she believed me. She laughed, and we held hands.

I was married to a woman in a church. We went home after the ceremony. The woman resembled my sister. We lay on the bed. We tried to have intercourse, but at first my organ did not enter, and it protruded from between her legs in the back.

My sister was slender. She wanted to have sex relations with me. I had a euphoric feeling.

My sister urgently needed a certain kind of food.

Childhood: Peer Relationships

I stole some electrical supplies from a house. Some teenage boys were there. I held a gun on them and told them to keep their distance, but they just ridiculed me.

I was with my mother and sister. We moved to another house. My mother asked me if I had any friends from our old neighborhood. I said I never had any except the Schnorr boys.

I was in a yard playing softball. I was not so good at it . . . In a later dream, my mother was playing catch in a gym. She was very good at it.

Identification with Children

I was on a porch with a boy and a girl. They were calling to a man.

I walked a short distance with a boy and a girl about eight years old, then I left them and went somewhere.

I was lying in the nude. Several girls about ten years old were around me. I became friendly with one of them. She seemed to be intelligent and creative, and have deep feelings. And she seemed to have compassion. As she sat next to me, I held her hand in mine, and I rested it on my organ. I tried my best to forbear having an erection. I did not at first feel that there was anything immoral about what we were doing. She seemed to be fascinated by my body. Then, a moment later, I had a slight feeling of guilt.

I left a department store and came into an alley. Some little girls were there, but I avoided them. I walked through a wooded area and saw more little girls on the path. They seemed carefree and gay. Two of them flashed their eyes at me. I noticed the legs of some others. I felt tempted to become friendly with them, but I resisted.

I formed a companionable relationship with a girl about ten.

A friendly black haired girl about ten spoke to me.

A girl with a voice like an eight year old was standing and posing for a picture on top of a table. But she was only a foot tall and looked like a doll. I marvelled that she was a live girl.

I was in a gym swinging on a rope with a little girl hanging on to me. We were enjoying ourselves.

Gender Confusion

. . . then he left, and reappeared dressed as a girl. At first I did not recognize him. . . . Then he laughed and I recognized his voice. He was acting as a girl in a play.

In the next dream a woman had breasts, but she had a male organ.

My sister and I hurried to catch a bus. My sister missed it. I saw her following the bus. Her dress was open in the center, exposing her body. She had a penis protruding from her sex organ.

I went into a rest room. There were men and women in there. A new ruling had been made allowing both men and women to use it. A woman tried to urinate in one of the men's urinals. I told her she would be better off using one of the commodes in the rear.

Failure of Control

I was standing on something a few feet above a man who was seated. I had to urinate and I did it there.

I had to urinate. I noticed that I was urinating on a repairman's coat, so I moved over.

Preoccupation with the Body: Interior Space

There was a large water pipe. I had to fix a leak.

Preoccupation with the Body: Writing and Printing

I was trying to get released from a hospital. In order to get released, I had to complete a test paper on writing and get a form signed by a woman.

I was writing stories. They had to be exciting.

I was writing stories. There was someone criticizing them. He said the adjectives were not strong enough. The sentences lacked nobility, emotion, spirit.

Fetal Identification

I was with my mother and sister in an amusement park. I wanted to go swimming in the gym, but I had to get my name on the member list. When I was allowed in the pool it was being emptied.

I wanted to get to an underground place. I had to sink through a noxious smelling fluid to get there.

Feminine Identification

I was fastened to a bed with a board across my legs, and my hands

were tied to the sides of the bed. I imagined that I had a woman tied there. . . At the same time I imagined that I was the victim.

I saw a girdle shaped like a dress form. I tried it on but it was too tight.

. . . I saw a pile of women's panties, and I started to try one on. Then I thought how silly I was so I put it down and tried on another pajama set.

Relationship to his Father

A bull that seemed to have human intelligence came behind me and held me against him. I did not like his advances, and I sensed that he wanted to have sex relations with me. So I broke away from him.

Appendix II

Rorschach Inkblot Test

	L	D	C	P-O
Card 1. (10 seconds) (1) I see two bears with their heads raised. Inquiry: It's the shape of the nose that makes me think of bears. They are looking up with their mouths closed.				
	d		F	A
(2) A profile of a character in a nursery rhyme, in a children's story. Inquiry: It's Pinocchio with his long nose, and he's looking straight ahead. The shape makes me think of him.	d		F	Hd
(3) This looks like a dog's head. Inquiry: It's the end part, the point of the nose, that reminds me of a dog. He's looking at something intently.	de		F	Ad

Card 1. (10 seconds) (1) I see two bears with their heads raised. Inquiry: It's the shape of the nose that makes me think of bears. They are looking up with their mouths closed. (2) A profile of a character in a nursery rhyme, in a children's story. Inquiry: It's Pinocchio with his long nose, and he's looking straight ahead. The shape makes me think of him. (3) This looks like a dog's head. Inquiry: It's the end part, the point of the nose, that reminds me of a dog. He's looking at something intently. (4) This little piece here looks like the side view of an African shouting. Inquiry: You can't see the top of his head. He's angry. Something about the shape, the big lips and the

head with no hair. (5) This looks like the nose and mouth of a man. Inquiry: It's definitely a man, not a woman. You can tell by the arrogant expression, the shape. He's	de, s	F	Hd
thinking. (6) It looks like the freakish dog with a boney head. The square nose makes it look like a St. Bernard. Inquiry: the shape, the fact that it has no ears makes it	S	F	Hd
look freakish. He's staring.	d	F	A
(7) They look like baby alligators with no teeth. Maybe it's a hippopotamus. Inquiry: the shape of the mouth. It's long.	d	F	A
(8) This reminds me of the top of the head of a frog. Inquiry: the shape of it. It's looking			
ahead. (9) This looks like a woman's torso, her dress form.	d	F	Ad
Inquiry: a woman's shape.	D	F	Hd

Card 2. (20 seconds) (1) These red
things look like women in a
children's story. Inquiry: they
are animals with a human
pose. They have a woman's
face. The rest is animals'
paws. They are conversing. I
can't place the story. It's the
facial features that make me

think so. (2) The red down here looks like a butterfly—this in the middle. Inquiry: here are the wings with a body in the center. It's in flight because a butterfly at	D	F	H→A

rest has its wings together.	D	FM	A

(3) Looks like the head of a spear.
Inquiry: because it's pointed.
It was done by hand, crude,
made by a savage. It's for

hunting and fighting. (4) The	S	F	Obj

side parts are like bears.
Inquiry: they are posing bears.
The shape of the nose and the

texture that looks like fur.	D	Fc	A	P

(5) A man laughing. Inquiry: I
can't locate it now. Oh, I see
it. The fact that the mouth is

open, it's shape.	de	F	H

Card 3. (10 seconds) (1) They are two	L	D	C	P-O

women dressed in slacks,
warming themselves at a fire.
Inquiry: their hands are
outstretched. They are women
because of the shape of their

breasts. (2) The middle part	D	M	H	P

reminds me of some kind of
organ in the human body.
Inquiry: they are lungs. You
can tell by the color tone, the

softness, the texture. (3) These	D	FC	At

on the side look like roosters
except for their long tail. The
comb is over here. Inquiry: I
guess it's the comb on the top,

its shape. (4) This is a	D	F	A

ferocious moose. Inquiry: just
the head. It's a female because
there aren't any horns. It's the
eye, the light spot shaped in
such a way that makes it look

ferocious. (5) These look like	D	F	A

two trees. Inquiry: the bottom

looks like a trunk. Just the shape. The texture is more like a mushroom. (6) In the middle it looks like a gray bat. It's partly obscured.	D	F	N
Inquiry: the shape, the ragged edges on the wings. It's flying.	D	FM	A

Card 4. (15 seconds) (1) The head of a rhinoceros although these end parts don't fit in. Inquiry: it's the shape of the eyes, they're looking straight ahead. D   FM Ad

(2) This looks like the end part, the tail features of a fowl, a chicken. Inquiry: it's shaped like a triangle. The texture also suggests the flesh of fowl. d   cF Ad

(3) These two look like snakes. It's hard to see anything mechanical; it's all from nature. Inquiry: the shape of the heads at the end. They are climbing up, going somewhere. (4) The tone of d   FM A
gray suggests wool, reminds me of sheep. Inquiry: the texture. Its mouth is open; it's moving, going somewhere. de C→FM A

(5) This reminds me of a man's face; there's the eye. Inquiry: the shape of the pursed lips. He's looking down and thinking about something. d   M Hd

Card 5. (5 seconds) (1) This looks like alligators. Inquiry: the shape. They're going after something. d   FM A

(2) The head of a bear with his
mouth open as if in pain.
Inquiry: the shape of the nose.
He's been injured. Look at the
lower part of the mouth; it's as
though he's crying out in pain. de   F   Ad
(3) This looks like a man's
head. He's lying on his back.
Inquiry: the shape reminds
me of a profile of a famous
man, maybe Lincoln. He's
reclining, looking up, a statue. de   M   Hd
(4) This also looks like a man
with a protruding forehead,
with an expression as though
he's angry. Inquiry: the shape
of the mouth suggests anger.
(5) They both look like de   F   Hd
pelicans with big bills.
Inquiry: the shape. They're
looking ahead. (6) These look d   FM   A
like two sides of meat, like a
leg of lamb. Inquiry: the
shape makes it look that way. d   F   AObj

Card 6. (10 seconds) (1) The hide of
an animal. It's been cut on one
side. The whole top part. It
looks like a rug. It's unusual
because the top of the head is
not in the center. Inquiry: the
shape of the sides makes it
look that way. (2) The gray D   A   AObj
part looks like a mound of
jello. Inquiry: first the texture,
then the shape of it. (3) A D   cF   Obj
dog's head with his nose up in
the air. Inquiry: the shape of

the nose and the top of the head. (4) Two profiles of a man with a beard and with something in his mouth. He's puffing out his cheeks. His beard is too low. Inquiry: the lighter shading in front makes it seem so. He has a whistle in his mouth, and he's blowing it. (5) That light gray looks like	d	F	A
part of an insect. Inquiry: the shape of the two nobs there.	de	M	Hd
It's just looking.	d	FM	Ad

Card 7. (10 seconds) (1) A female bunny rabbit in a comic strip. Inquiry: the shape of the ears. Looks like Bugs Bunny's girl friend. It's just looking. (2) An animal that, by the shape of his mouth with the teeth and nose, looks angry. It's almost like a human; the eyes look human. Inquiry: the shape. It's going to do something violent. (3) A moth. Inquiry: it's softness; it's too soft to be a butterfly. The moth is resting. (4) The middle part looks like a skunk with a streak down its back. Inquiry: the light streak in the center. It is standing and looking. (5) A man's profile. He's shouting about something. Inquiry: the shape of the head. He's warning somebody.

friend. It's just looking. (2) An	D	FM	A
violent. (3) A moth. Inquiry:	D	F	A
resting. (4) The middle part	D	F	A
It is standing and looking.	d	FM	A
warning somebody.	D	M	Hd

Card 8. (20 seconds) (1) The pink and yellow part looks like a butterfly. Inquiry: the shape of the wings. It's lighting on something or getting ready to fly. (2) These two on the sides   D   F   A look like polar bears. Inquiry: the texture and shape. They're climbing something. (3) This   D   FM   A   P here is a vampire or bat. Its texture, not so much the shape. Inquiry: its texture and shape. It's flying. (4) Two   D   FM   A insects pushing against something. Inquiry: the shape of the legs. (5) The center is   D   F   A an insect being pushed by the other two insects. Inquiry: the shape of it.   di   F   A

Card 9. (5 seconds) (1) Two characters in a children's story. They're blowing a horn or a flute. Inquiry: the shape. I can't recall the rhyme. The Norse God Thor, of thunder, powerful, and sitting on a cloud. (2) An animal's head, an   D   F   H anteater. Inquiry: its pointed nose. It's looking up. (3) The   de   FM   Ad bottom part looks like a buffalo. Just the head and body, no legs. Inquiry: the dark part in the center, its head. Also the shape of the whole area. It has a big thorax.   di   C^{1}F Ad (4) A candle burning here.

There's a flame on the top, a
glow. Inquiry: the shape of
the flame. (5) These are   D   Fm   Obj
openings in something made
of wax. The dark parts are the
thickness of it. Inquiry: the
white and the dark green
makes it look softer than
stone, more like a wax candle.
It's round. (6) An old man with D,S   cF   Obj
a handlebar mustache.
Inquiry: the shape of the
forehead and nose. It's a
character from the roaring
'20's. He's on his back,
looking out.   D   F   Hd

Card 10. (5 seconds) (1) Two squids.
They're angry. Inquiry: the
shape of the legs at the
bottom. They're in conflict
with each other. (2) The blue   D   F   A
area here looks like a spider.
Inquiry: the shape of the legs.
It's moving toward the center
of the picture. (3) The blue in D   FM   A   P
the center looks like raccoons.
Inquiry: the dark part. They're
staring. (4) These look like   D   C   A
dwarfs in children's stories,
the dwarf named Grumpy.
Inquiry: the shape of the
forehead with small facial
features and a grumpy
expression. (5) Deer jumping   di   F   H
into the air. Inquiry: the shape
of the head that's raised and
the outstretched legs. (6) Two   D   FM   A

shrimp. Inquiry: their shape.
They are moving. (7) The   D   FM   A
yellow part looks like a bird
with an eye, and a beak
protruding down. Inquiry: the
shape. The bill is the pointed
part. It's staring. (8) Two   D   F   A
berries hanging from a branch.
Inquiry: the shape of the two
round pieces.   D   F   Nat.

Total Responses (R) = 60
Average Reaction Time (1, 4, 5, 6, 7) = 10 seconds
Average Reaction Time (2, 3, 7, 9, 10) = 10 seconds

$$\frac{\text{Total F}}{R} = \frac{31}{60} = 51\%$$

$$\frac{Fk+F+Fc}{R} = \frac{37}{60} = 61\%$$

$$\frac{A+Ad}{R} = \frac{36}{60} = 60\%$$

Number of P = 4

Number of 0 = 0

(H+A) (Hd+Ad) = (31) : (18) = 1.7:1

$$\text{Sum C} = \frac{FC+2CF+3C}{2} = \frac{2+8+3}{2} = 6.5$$

M:sum C = 5:6.5 = 1:1.3

(FM+m) : (Fc+c+C^1) = (16+0) : (1) = 16:1

$$\frac{\text{No. of R's to 8,9,10}}{R} = \frac{19}{60} = 31\%$$

W:M = 0:5

Thematic Apperception Test

1. The boy is learning the violin. He doesn't have much hope for being successful. He's not interested in it, not doing it willingly. He's filled with boredom. He doesn't know what to do to better his situation; it has no meaning. He can't have new parents, and, therefore, the situation will remain the same: he will probably always be a failure. He won't do anything violent or drastic; he'll vent his feelings among his friends, and this will be his outlet. He's not introverted. I have the feeling he's being exploited.

2. The young girl, or lady, is a student. She doesn't like the simple life of the farm. The man is her brother; the woman is her mother. The mother is contented. But her daughter has deep feelings, and she'll do what she wants no matter what her mother says. She's interested in some career. There's no father here. Her mother is insensitive, self-centered; she'll do what's best for herself and won't grieve about anything. Her daughter will be loyal to her husband if she gets married. She has moral courage.

3 BM. A woman has shot herself (see the gun on the floor). Everything seemed absurd to her; nothing seemed important. The world will be the same without her. She didn't have much money, and her clothes were poor. She was just a burden. She's not dead yet (look at the position of the body), but she has resigned herself to dying.

4. The man is planning to embark on an enterprise of some kind, and the woman is trying to dissuade him. He wants to do something risky, and she's afraid she'll lose him, that something will happen to him. It may be a criminal activity of some sort.

He's determined to do what he wants to do. He's not the romantic type and, therefore, not much influenced by her.

5. This middle aged woman has been through a trial of some kind, either physical or mental suffering. She's reflecting on something as she looks into the room. The room reminds her of what took place there, some kind of violence which was the climax of a long conflict. She seems depressed about the future and will never take an interest in anything for the rest of her life.

6 BM. The son is in legal trouble. He's going to court and anticipating a decision. His mother is worried about the outcome. He'd been involved in embezzling because he needed money for a woman he loved. His mother is in a state of shock by what he did, but they have fortitude and will make the best of the outcome.

7 BM. The young man feels he's been treated injustly, and he's vindictive about it. The older man is morally depraved, and he's suggesting a plan by which the young man can avenge himself. The young man is thinking about it. It seems that some male acquaintance of his had deceived him. He lacks moral courage. He will choose to revenge himself rather than exposing the one who deceived him.

8 BM. The boy is thinking about what is in the background: a gun there, a war or something, a man who has to be operated on. It's a memory of something he saw in the past. Even though the man was close to him, he's not sympathetic; it's just a memory without emotions. It affected him emotionally, but he's repressed it. The incident will affect him throughout his lifetime, his judgments and decisions and his relationships with other people. He

will present an apathetic front toward other people, but this is only on the surface; underneath there is a tender feeling. It was a physical conflict, a war of some kind. The son was there when the man was operated on, and the operation was not successful.

9 BM. There's a colored man there, a husky white man, and a more slender one looking away from the picture. Oh, there's another one, a fourth, lying on his stomach. They are only interested in the basic needs of life. They're concerned (by their expressions) with asserting themselves in a manly way; they won't let anyone push them around. They're just resting. By their dress I would say they are either migrant workers or else they pick up odd jobs. Afterwards they will travel to look for work in a plantation.

10. They are a husband and wife, both the same age; you can tell they are married by the way they're embracing. The husband is trying to express his care for her. They have known each other a long time. They are very sincere. (The subject appears to have a difficult time with this card.) The wife needed some consolation. She'd felt deserted by one of her children. She'll be all right; she'll recover.

11. I see two buffalo on a ledge. It's something like inkblots, hard to figure out. On the side of the cliff there's a cave where a bird is resting. The bird is strange: it doesn't have feathers, it has skin like a frog, and cloven feet, and a bill like a duck. It is looking out at the buffalo, watching to see if there's any danger. Behind the buffalo there is a small boy going in the opposite direction (to the right), cross-

ing a man-made bridge to the other side, across the gorge. He is running. He has nothing to do with the buffalo, just hurrying some place before it gets dark. It doesn't seem as though he'll make it since his destination is not near by.

12 M. It is hard to tell the emotion from the man's face. He seems to be studying her. He is younger than her, and she is his older sister. He probably has a leering smile on his face; he's been experimenting in some way, and his sister is part of his experiment. There is likely to be a showdown when she finds out about him, and they will probably separate.

13 MF. The books on the table there belong to him. He is a studious person who was charmed by her, and now he regrets what he did. He is disillusioned about the situation. She's older than he is, and this is probably his first intimacy with a woman. It's not going to turn out very well, and he's not going to be able to cope with the situation.

14. He's looking upwards out the window and thinking about plans for the future. He's hopeful, and confident in his ability to achieve what he hopes to do. He's about twenty years old, and he'll succeed because he's young and has handsome features. He would make a good leader.

15 BM. He's sliding down the wall, outside the corner of the wall. He's probably above some water (by the way he's undressed). He is escaping from somewhere, and he's going to swim. He seems to be very confident that no one will be able to stop him, and he's strong enough to endure hardships. He is not an educated person (from his features) but is crafty; he's good at something mechanical.

Adjective Check List

	Standard Score	
		50
Number Checked	51	
Favorable	62	
Unfavorable	57	
Defensiveness	48	
Self-Confidence	47	
Self-Control	43	
Lability	51	
Personal Adjustment	41	
Need:		
Achievement	50	
Dominance	39	
Endurance	40	
Order	43	
Intraception	64	
Nurturance	48	
Affiliation	45	
Heterosexuality	31	
Exhibition	33	
Autonomy	46	
Aggression	44	
Change	61	
Succorance	49	
Abasement	57	
Deference	54	
Counseling Readiness	63	

Bills Index of Adjustment and Values

1. Sum of Self-Descriptive Adjectives: 180
   Self-Ideal Discrepancy: 25
   Self-Mother Discrepancy: 53
   Self-Father Discrepancy: 42
   Ideal-Mother Discrepancy: 51
   Ideal-Father Discrepancy: 62
   Mother-Father Discrepancy: 56

2. Self Description
   Most of the time: broad-minded, teachable, studious, sincere, reasonable.

   Much less often: competitive, merry, helpful, economical, acceptable.

3. Mother Description
   Most of the time: accurate, ambitious, busy, confident, dependable, economical, helpful, purposeful, sincere, competitive.

   Much less often: academic, studious.

4. Father Description
   Most of the time: unafraid

   Much less often: ambitious, democratic, economical, friendly, fashionable, helpful, kind, merry, optimistic, studious.

The Personality of a Child Molester
Edwards Personal Preference Schedule

Percentile

1 10 20 30 40 50 60 70 80 90 99

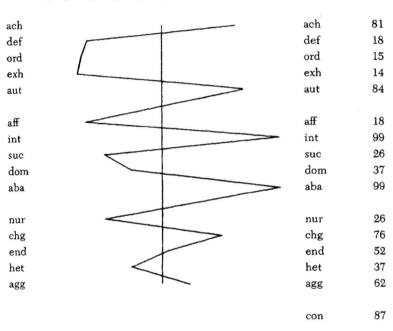

ach	81
def	18
ord	15
exh	14
aut	84
aff	18
int	99
suc	26
dom	37
aba	99
nur	26
chg	76
end	52
het	37
agg	62
con	87

The Minnesota Multiphasic Personality Inventory

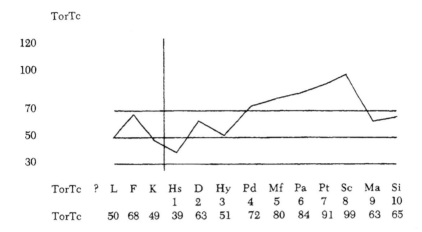

TorTc	?	L	F	K	Hs	D	Hy	Pd	Mf	Pa	Pt	Sc	Ma	Si
					1	2	3	4	5	6	7	8	9	10
TorTc		50	68	49	39	63	51	72	80	84	91	99	63	65

Incomplete Sentences Blank–Adult Form

I like to daydream about majestic, enduring structures.

The happiest time is the time of opportunity.

I want to know unknown truths.

Back home in _____, a bank building filled me with awe.

I regret that I find it so hard to distinguish my needs from my whims.

At bedtime I sometimes experience a vague fear.

Men should value competence above physical prowess.

The best is what is most good, not what is most useful.

What annoys me is ridicule of values that I believe are true.

People should be ends in themselves, not means to an end.

A mother is a link between the past and the future.

I feel a keen and sometimes terrifying sense of time.

My greatest fear is just punishment.

In school I liked to study grammar.

I can't both run with the rabbit and hunt with the hounds.

Sports are a form of warfare. Hunting is predatory.

When I was a child, God seemed very majestic at Christmas time.

My nerves could be integrated completely with my brain waves.

Other people sometimes appear more dedicated than I am.

I suffer when I seem unable to acquire more depth.

I failed to give direction to my life when I was a youth.

Reading inspiring works is like experiencing a beautiful light.

My mind is not my intellect, but my imagination.

The future is eternal, and so is the past.

I need a higher consciousness.

Marriage is sacred, because the sacred evolution of man is possible only by biological reproduction.

I am best when I feel a contact with the supernatural.

Sometimes emotional equilibrium seems unattainable.

What pains me most is a feeling of having lost my life's meaning.

I hate unwarranted criticism of myself and others.

This place that I call my body sometimes bewilders me.

I am very attracted to pleasure, but it does not make me happy.

The only trouble with attaining will power is that tenderness is sacrificed.

I wish that my life had a more revealed direction.

My father had an air of dignity about him which often made me afraid and ponderous.

I secretly wish I had a taller, more majestic body like my father's body.

I believe philosophy has saved me from dispair.

Dancing makes me feel less afraid of time, and more in rythmn (sic) with it.

My greatest worry is evil, how to recognize it, and what to do with it.

Most women are as competent as men.

Wechsler Adult Intelligence Scale

SUMMARY

TEST	Raw Score	Scaled Score
Information	25	15
Comprehension	27	19
Arithmetic	15	14
Similarities	19	13
Digit Span	17	19
Vocabulary	67	15
Verbal Score		95
Digit Symbol	60	11
Picture Completion	19	14
Block Design	46	15
Picture Arrangement	27	11
Object Assembly	37	12
Performance Score		63

TOTAL SCORE: 158

Verbal Score	95	IQ	134
Performance Score	63	IQ	122
Full Scale Score	158	IQ	131

Study of Values

Profile of Values

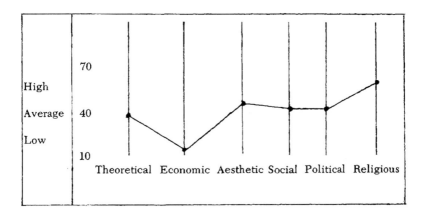

Index

9 781412 818476